RESILIENT
My Story, God's Glory
A Memoir

RESILIENT
My Story, God's Glory
A Memoir

**ROBIN
TERRY**

ARI SYMONE PUBLISHING

Resilient: My Story, God's Glory
Copyright © 2019 by Robin Terry

All rights reserved. No part of this book may be reproduced, scanned, stored in a retrieval system, or distributed in any printed, electronic, mechanical, or photocopy form- except for brief quotations in printed reviews without written permission from the publisher.

Unless otherwise noted, all Scripture quotations are taken from the Holman Christian Standard Bible®, Used by Permission HCSB ©1999,2000,2002,2003,2009 Holman Bible Publishers. Holman Christian Standard Bible®, Holman CSB®, and HCSB® are federally registered trademarks of Holman Bible Publishers.

Scripture taken from the New King James Version®. Copyright © 1982 by Thomas Nelson. Used by permission. All rights reserved.

First Printed: February 2020 / Printed in the United States of America

ISBN: 978-1-7333988-2-4 (Hardback)

ISBN: 978-1-7333988-1-7 (E-book)

ISBN: 978-1-7333988-0-0 (Paperback)

Library of Congress Control Number: 2019919002

Photographer: Susan Heard Photography
Cover Design: 5MediaDesign

To my darling Ariel, being your mother has been one of the greatest joys of my life. You are my sunshine! To my strong and beautiful mother, thank you for always being there for me. You are the most precious jewel I'll ever know.

Contents

Preface

xi

Resilient through Rejection

5

Resilient through Unwise Choices

95

Resilient through Pain

139

Resilient through Deception

191

Resilient through Fear

229

Afterword

280

Acknowledgements

283

Robin Terry

Some names and identifying details have been changed to protect the privacy of individuals.

Robin Terry

I remember it just like it was yesterday…

Robin Terry

Resilient

1/24/1998

Dear Journal,

Yesterday, I lost my virginity and sex was not as good as I thought it was going to be. All I could feel during the entire act was numb. There was no emotion or love felt like the people in the movies. On TV, they made it seem like sex was awesome, and it would be the best experience of my life. I beg to differ; it sucked. My eyes weren't rolling in the back of my head. I felt no magic, no spark. It didn't feel good. When Austin was done, I got up and went into the house. Blood was all over my stomach and legs. It was like I was having my period for the last time. I thought I would feel like a woman, but all I feel is shame and disgust with myself. It was nothing like I imagined it would be. Austin got more pleasure out of this horrible experience than I did. I mean, really? I'm so pissed. Not only that, I feel like I disappointed my mom. In the back of mind, she was screaming, "Don't do it!" Or was it God? Either way, something was trying to keep me from making a mistake. Truth is, I didn't want to, but Austin kept asking and pushing the issue. He didn't force me, but he sure as hell got on my nerves about sex until I gave in. At first, he was like, "I wanna fuck you so bad." When I asked him to repeat himself, he changed his tune and said, "I wanna make love to you. You're so pure." I should have known right then what the real deal was, but I stayed in the relationship and kept talking to him even though it made me uncomfortable.

After about a month and a half of him bringing it up, I went along with it. I almost lost my nerve yesterday. Then I asked my sister, Dionne, what I should do. She said, "I don't know, but if you do, you need to use a condom." I didn't have any condoms, and neither did Austin. He said he didn't want to use one and sex would feel better without it. When I look back on it, that should have been a red flag. How would he know when he had told me that he was still a virgin? Anyway, I agreed; we were both virgins. What's the worst that could happen?

    I went outside in a t-shirt and a pair of panties. It was dark outside so my next-door neighbor Cynthia, who also happens to be my cousin, couldn't see me. It was between 6:00 and 6:30 in the evening. It was the perfect time; Austin was supposed to pick up Dionne and me to meet our mom at Pizza Hut around 7:30. Well, I got into his green mustang. As soon as I got in, he started kissing and licking on me right away. I wanted to take a moment to think, but it was like he knew I would change my mind or something. It was all going along too fast. Before I knew it, he laid me down on the backseat and was bumping and grinding away. He didn't give my body time to adjust to him. I couldn't feel much. I just felt pain, and then I was numb. I guess the whole act lasted a few minutes or so. It wasn't that long.

    At fifteen years old, I don't know what making love is, but I'm almost positive it should be a little slower and more sensual, pleasurable even. He didn't take his time with me at all. No wonder there was blood everywhere.

    Anyway, I pretended to be happy and pleased in his presence, but I was really upset and thinking what the hell did I just do? I felt different, like a piece of me had just gone missing. What was it? Who am I now? Am I the same person? I got out of the car and ran into the house straight to the bathroom to look in the mirror.

Resilient

I looked the same, but I felt strange like something was off. Austin waited outside while I cleaned myself up. I told Dionne about my experience and the blood. All she said was, "I hope you used a condom." When I was ready, Dionne and I went outside to get in the car to leave. Before going to Pizza Hut, we stopped by JB's house. He's one of Austin's friends that lives on the other side of town. Austin had taken his t-shirt off to clean up the inside of the car while I was in the house because blood had also gotten on the backseat. He asked JB for a hot towel to finish cleaning up what the t-shirt didn't get. JB immediately knew what had gone down by what he saw. I was completely embarrassed; that wasn't anything I wanted anyone else to know. When we left there, we drove to Pizza Hut. The ride there was awkward for me. I didn't have much to say. I was still drowning in my thoughts.

When we walked inside Pizza Hut, Mama was already there. We sat down with her to eat. Some of our friends from school were there, but I went to my mom instead. She kept staring at me like she knew what I had done. Then she said something really weird to me. "You look different. What's going on?" I wanted to melt into the floor. How could she know?

I glanced up at her and said, "Nothing, just sleepy," hoping she wouldn't see through my lie. I knew she knew I was lying because a mother always knows. But she dropped it and changed the subject. Thank the Lord! Now all I can say is Father, please forgive me, and please don't let me be pregnant. It seemed like all of that blood was a sign. I'm only fifteen, and I don't want a baby. Amen.

Resilient

I am the youngest of four children. I have an older brother and two older sisters. I grew up in a town called West Point, MS; the smallest of two larger towns that make up the Golden Triangle. The Golden Triangle consists of West Point, Columbus, and Starkville, MS. In small-town West Point during the '80s and '90s, there were smaller communities where both good and bad news spread quickly. It was a blessing and a curse. As a young child, I heard a lot of things I shouldn't have heard. I saw a lot of things I wish I had not seen.

For the first nine years of my life, my mother was a single parent. She was in a relationship with my dad, but they weren't married. My mom had a three-bedroom with one-bathroom apartment she was raising the four of us in. We lived in low-income subsidy housing, in a neighborhood called Dunlap Acres. My sisters and I shared one room. My brother had his room to himself. My mother had the third bedroom. Mama raised all of us to love and care for one another. She always said, "When I'm dead and gone, you'll only have each other. So, love each other and take care of each other." Our home was filled with a lot of love. Mama did the best that she could to take care of us. She had incredible strength.

During my early childhood, I watched my mother work to support our family and go to nursing school. She would get up at five o'clock in the morning to go to class. I remember one day when I was maybe seven or eight years old, I saw mama at the kitchen table crying. I went over to comfort her. I wanted to know what was wrong. She told me that her professor failed her. The class was one that she needed to move forward in the program to start clinical training. I felt so bad for her. Although Mama could have quit because she was discouraged, she kept going. She applied to

Itawamba Community College in Fulton, MS to start their nursing program. Mama had to commute about an hour to and from class on most days of the week. Mama later graduated with her nursing degree; all while raising four children on her own. That is how I learned what perseverance looked like.

My dad was raised a country boy, turned mechanic, turned carpenter. Daddy worked just as hard as Mama did. He worked while he went to college to help cover his tuition. As my grandmother's only living son, he made sure Grandma had what she needed. He was the man of the house and had been for a long time. Daddy went to college at Mississippi State University. He later got accepted into the University of Mississippi College of Pharmacy. He was as busy as Mama was; he worked on cars, school buses, houses, and various other projects all while attending college. My dad was well-known by a lot of people in our small town. He was also an ordained deacon in the church and a Sunday School teacher. Daddy graduated from pharmacy school in the early '90s.

I learned what strength, perseverance, and resilience looked like from both parents. So, failure wasn't an option for me. I worked hard in school to make good grades. I wanted to be the best student in the class. I was competitive when it came to my grades. It was how my friends and I pushed each other to excel. By the time I got to junior high, I knew I was going to college. I also knew that I wanted to be in healthcare. I was torn between following my dad's footsteps to become a pharmacist or going to medical school. Though I noticed boys and wanted to date a little, I was more focused on school and enjoying life.

When I was in eighth grade, Austin wanted to court me, but I wasn't interested. There was another boy I liked. His name was

Resilient

Alex. I had the biggest crush on Alex. He was so cute with his black wavy hair and smooth brown skin. I didn't think of any other boys; only Alex. By the time I was allowed to date, the crush I had on Alex was long gone. Eventually, I started dating Austin. My relationship with Austin was one that changed my life as I knew it, forever.

Resilient

Resilient through Rejection…

Robin Terry

1

After I gave away the most precious thing I had, Austin and I remained in a relationship for a little while longer, but things were different. He still held my hand at school, and we even talked on the phone. We still hung out together, but everything had changed. Our relationship was no longer innocent love. It was no longer what I would call 'puppy love.' He brought up sex even more since we had done it already. I still didn't feel too comfortable doing it because it felt wrong, so I blew him off and changed the subject when he brought it up. We did have sex one more time. I had convinced my mom to let me go over to Tyra's, my oldest sister, apartment. He came over, and we had a quickie while she was in the shower. After we finished having sex, I noticed a fishy odor. I thought it was weird, but I didn't say anything about it to Austin. I don't know if he noticed it or not, but I did. Mama always taught me to pay attention to my body because if something is not right, I should be the first person to know. At that moment, I knew something was not right. I just didn't know what it was. After Austin was gone, my mom picked me up to take me home later that night. When I got in the car, as always, she knew something wasn't right. She asked me, "What is that smell? I smell fish." *How did she know these things?* I told her my sister had cooked some fish, and that was the end of it.

Over the next several days, I woke up, got dressed, went to school, gave the teacher my attention in class, went home, took a nap, got up to do homework, ate dinner, did my chores, and went to bed again. I repeated this cycle every day. It's like someone had put me on autopilot, and I was going through the motions. It was time for my period around the first week of February, but I was spotting a lot. Mama asked me if my period had started because she kept up with it. I told her yes, neglecting to mention I was only spotting. *No need to worry her or me, right?* I was hoping that I wasn't pregnant; that would be an awful thing. First off, my parents would kill me. There was no way I could take care of a baby. I couldn't even take care of myself, which made me regret January 23 more and more. Oh, how I wished I had just said no that day. Why in the hell didn't I go with my gut and say, "Hell to the no! I'm not ready, and you can't pressure me." I felt stupid.

Furthermore, what really had me upset was that the blood from my period was a dark reddish-brown color, and it had a foul odor. The smell was horrible. I didn't even want to go to the bathroom to pee. There was no way I could tell my mother about it because then she would know I'd had sex with someone. There was no way I could tell anybody. I was too embarrassed to say anything to Lillie or Shanda, my best friends, and too ashamed to tell my mother. All I could do was pray to the good Lord that it would all go away.

I wished a thousand times I could turn back the hands of time. I would do that dreadful day differently. I would've changed everything. But, in life, we learn that we can't undo what's already been done. I would have to suffer whatever the consequences would be. Austin had been distant toward me since the last time we had sex. I couldn't even bring myself to tell him what was going on with me. It was almost as if he didn't want to have anything else to do with me. I should have known that would happen; my mama warned my sisters and me about this very thing. She would always say, "Keep the door of the church closed. Keep the lock on your pocketbook," and one of my favorites, "Don't let everybody see your feet." When we were disobedient, she would say, "A hard head makes a soft ass." I must say, my ass was feeling mighty soft.

One day, I remember I was at school, and I couldn't get the thought of being pregnant out of my head. I walked into class, took my seat behind Lillie, and I whispered in her ear, "If I tell you something, do you promise not to tell anybody?" I knew I shouldn't have told her, but I had to talk to someone to get the heaviness off my chest.

"I promise," she said, as she leaned to her left side to hear.

"I think I might be pregnant," I blurted out. Lillie looked at me in disbelief, and then said, "I knew this was going to happen."

"How did you know?"

"Because you kept talking about doing it with him. Why didn't you use a condom?"

"I don't know. I didn't think I would get pregnant. I counted the days on the calendar. I must have counted it wrong. Plus, he didn't want to use a condom." She shook her head from side to side in disapproval. I couldn't say anything more. My sister had warned me about the same thing, but I didn't listen. God, why didn't I listen? Was I that desperate to please a boy?

"What are you gonna do?"

"Honestly, I don't know," I said through tears. We were at school. I couldn't wail the way I wanted to without all the other kids around noticing. I wanted to let out all of my pent-up frustrations. But I couldn't, not at school and not at home. Lillie could probably tell I was about to explode. She said, "Maybe it's just stress, Robin. Don't freak out yet."

"Okay." Maybe she was right. There was no need to freak out yet. At least I was spotting some blood. That's a good sign, right? Although I was hoping it was a good sign, deep down I knew it wasn't.

The bell rang, indicating it was time for class to start. I quickly gathered my thoughts so I could pay attention in class. I loved my French teacher, Mrs. Portnoy and the class. When class was over, Lillie and I walked out together, heading to our lockers.

On our way, I saw Austin in the hallway with his friends laughing and joking around. He was dressed in khakis and a red polo shirt. He was fine at about five-seven, smooth golden skin, and a smile with straight white teeth to die for. His hair was freshly cut, and he was feeling himself that day. He looked good, and he knew it. He looked at me and turned his head like I wasn't even there. Before he got in my panties, he would rush over to help me with my books or stand with me at my locker. Then, he had the nerve to act like he didn't even see me.

"Did you see that?" I asked Lillie.

"Sure did. He has some nerve; that's cold."

Resilient

"I ought to go over there and slap the taste out his mouth!"

"No, girl, don't worry about it. Just act like you don't see him either." She was exactly right. Why should I make a scene in front of everyone for a boy who clearly wasn't as into me as I thought he was?

Valentine's Day was just a few days away, and I was hoping everything would get better for us. When I ran into Austin at the end of the school day, while walking out to catch the bus home, I was still feeling stupid. I had not talked to him in a while; it was kind of awkward. We stared at each other, me in disbelief, and him in…what? Disregard maybe. *Is this dude going to speak to me or what?* With frustration, I spoke up first.

"Hey"

"What's up?" he asked, displaying a blank expression. I was trying to read him, but I couldn't. I didn't know what he was going to say next.

"Why have you been ignoring me?" I blurted out.

"I haven't been ignoring you!" He said, a bit too loudly and with too much attitude.

"Yes, you have! You were acting like you didn't even see me the other day when you were with your boys, and you haven't returned any of my phone calls!" By then, I was pissed off and didn't mind letting him know it.

"Whatever, dude."

"Whatever, dude?" I couldn't believe what I'd just heard.

"Look, I'm just tired of you okay," he said, looking away. He looked to the left of my face, then down at the floor. Without saying another word, he stalked off.

I was stunned, speechless. It felt like the wind was knocked out of me. I was deeply hurt. I willingly gave Austin my virginity. I stayed up many nights, losing sleep while talking on the phone with him. I went against my gut instinct and everything my parents taught me to give him what he wanted. Then, he said he was tired of me. How could this be happening to me? What the hell had just happened? It was over just as fast as it had begun. I felt like such a fool. Valentine's Day was right around the corner. Not only would I not be receiving a Valentine's gift from the one guy I thought loved me, but I could also be pregnant and would be raising the child alone.

I didn't want to go to school over the next couple of weeks. I had some of my friends ask me what happened between Austin and me. I told them exactly what he said. Mom asked, but I was too ashamed to tell her. So, I just told her we broke up. I assumed she didn't want to pry because she didn't ask me anything else about it. Although I was upset about it, I tried not to let it control me. I couldn't keep my mind off of the fact that I wouldn't feel as bad as I felt if I had not had sex with him.

***

It was early March. The weather was mild that day. When I got home from school, I was tired. I went directly to my room to take a nap. As I was dozing off to sleep, I heard my sister, Dionne, sweeping the hallway floor. She woke me up when she saw Mama coming into the driveway. She was home early from work. Mama worked as a registered nurse in the emergency department of the county hospital in Starkville. Starkville, MS, a small city, is the home of the Mississippi State University Bulldogs. The drive from

Resilient

West Point to Starkville is about twenty minutes or so.

In a panic, I jumped from my twin-sized bed and hurried to make up Mama and Daddy's bed. Cleaning up my parents' room was part of my to-do list every day. I hated to clean up their room, but they never knew it. Their room was a decent size with a queen-sized bed and nightstands on each side of the bed. There was also carpet, so I had to vacuum and dust. And there was an en-suite bathroom, which I also had to clean up every day.

When Mama walked into the house, I was already in her room cleaning up. She had no reason to think I had been napping. As Mama walked into the bedroom, I greeted her with a smile.

"Hey, Mama!"

"Hi, Robin. I'm going to take a shower. I'm not feeling too good."

"What's wrong?" I hated it when my mama was sick. She looked so pitiful; so unlike herself.

"It was something I ate at work. I had tuna salad. It must have been bad. I'll never eat it at work again."

"You need anything?"

"Yeah. Go get me some water and an Alka-Seltzer." Alka-Seltzer was and still is Mama's go-to medication for stomach aches and indigestion.

I went upstairs to do what Mama asked me to do. Yes, the kitchen is upstairs. My daddy built our home that way. For whatever reason, he loved the four bedrooms, two-and-a-half bathrooms, split-level floor plan when he found it and decided to build it. The kitchen, dining room, and living area are all upstairs. The den is on the lowest level of our home with the two-door garage. Some found it hard to believe; but, yes, my daddy built our home himself. Not only was my dad a pharmacist, he was also by trade, a carpenter and mechanic. He was the general contractor and builder of his dream home. I was always proud of that.

I remember how much I loved going to the site as the house was being built. My daddy was my hero. I saw how strong and smart he was to be able to do that. I watched him and his contracting buddies in amazement. I loved the smell of the wood and the sounds of the hammers and drills. He wouldn't let me get too close because he said it was dangerous. So, I watched from afar. In my eyes, my father could do no wrong. He was the king of my life as far as I was concerned. I was the ultimate daddy's girl. In some ways now, I still am. Once, I asked him if he would build my house when I grew up. He just laughed and said, "I'll be too old then."

By the time I made it back downstairs, Mama had already gotten in the shower. When she got out of the bathroom, I gave her the Alka-Seltzer I had prepared. She drank it down in a few gulps and headed to her favorite green recliner to rest. I decided to go ahead and iron my clothes for the next day of school. The ironing board and iron were always in my parents' closet; I would get them out and iron in their room.

While I was ironing, my mom was staring at me. It made me a little uncomfortable. I tried to ignore it. Every time I looked up, she was staring at me. I was just a bit worried by it, but I didn't say anything, hoping she would look away. Then, out of nowhere, she said, "Robin, are you having sex?"

I was like a deer caught in the headlights. I was stunned. I replied, "No ma'am."

"Don't lie to me. You know I don't like being lied to. Now, I'm going to ask you one more time. Are you having sex?" This time her voice was more forceful. I decided it would be in my best interest to tell the truth.

"Well, it was only one time." I was nervous; my voice was shaking. I didn't want to tell her about the second time I'd had sex. The first experience was bad enough. I held my breath while waiting for her to flip out on me. To my surprise, she didn't. She asked me a follow-up question.

"When did you have sex?"

"January 23."

"You're pregnant," she said matter-of-factly.

"No, I'm not!" I nearly yelled. My heart was about to jump out of my chest at the accusation. I could not believe my mom could look at me and say such a thing.

"Yes, you are," she responded with authority. She flipped up the calendar hanging on the wall next to her recliner. She looked at the days and said, "You are pregnant, and you were ovulating that day." I stood there looking like a fool. I could have sworn I counted my days correctly, so there would be no chance of me getting pregnant. I still had hope I wasn't pregnant up until that moment. The pit of my stomach felt like it hit the floor; I was speechless. What could I say? What could I do to change things? To my dismay, there wasn't a damn thing I could do about what my mom revealed to me. She knew with all certainty that I was carrying a baby.

She picked up the phone and called my oldest sister, Tyra.

"Hi, Tyra, go to the store and buy a pregnancy test."

Tyra was asking questions because Mama said, "Just do what I said; we will talk later." Then Mama disconnected the call. She put the phone down, and said, "Maybe I'm wrong. Let's just wait and see what the test says."

My sister arrived a little while later with my nephew and the pregnancy test in tow. Tyra walked in and said, "Who's pregnant?"

"Don't worry about it," Mama said, hurrying Tyra out of the house. "I'll call you later."

As soon as Tyra was gone, Mama gave me the box holding the pregnancy test. Tyra picked up the E.P.T test, which I assumed was one of the most accurate tests available. I held the box in my hand, staring at it, knowing that in a matter of minutes, the course of my life would depend on whether or not the test was positive or negative. Mama snapped me out of my reverie and hurried me to the bathroom. Once in the bathroom, I stood there for a minute or so, looking at myself in the mirror. I was wondering what I was going to do if the test turned out to be positive.

Mama was very disappointed when Tyra got pregnant. I saw how upset she was. Mama got pregnant when she was eighteen years old with Tyra. I know that is not something she wanted for any of her girls. She didn't want us to be unwed mothers. She didn't want our lives to be harder than they needed to be. Since she was upset when Tyra got pregnant, I just knew she was going to explode if I turned out to be pregnant.

I turned the box over and read the directions. With shaking hands, I opened the box and removed the test. I removed my clothing and urinated on the end of the stick, replaced the cap, and placed it face up, as directed, on the top of the toilet. I washed my hands and opened the bathroom door. Mom and Dionne were standing in the hallway waiting for me to come out. I was trying to read their faces to see how they were feeling. If they were as nervous as I was, it didn't show. I stood in the bathroom with the door open, looking at them. I felt nothing but fear and anticipation. I felt like my legs were going to give out; I was so nervous.

After about a minute or two, Mama came in and picked up the stick. She looked at it; then handed it to me. I didn't want to look at it because deep down inside, I already knew the results, but I looked at it anyway. There it was, two blue lines indicating I was pregnant. I was speechless. Dionne asked, "What does it say?" I looked at her and gave her the test. She looked at it, and then she grabbed the box to make sure she interpreted the results correctly. Shock was written all over her face.

I started to cry, and so did Mama and Dionne. "I'm sorry, Mama," I wailed. I couldn't stop those tears from falling. I was afraid. I never expected anything like this to happen to me.

"It's going to be all right," Mama said, wiping my tears away. She hugged me and held me close as I cried in her arms. Dionne came and hugged me from behind. All three of us stood there in the bathroom, embracing each other, crying. Mama pulled back for just a moment and asked me a question I didn't expect.

"Do you want to get rid of it?"

With tears streaming, it took me only a moment to say, "You didn't get rid of me." Those were words I didn't expect to come out of my mouth; but to my surprise, they did.

"Okay, I was just checking to see where your mind is," she said. I don't remember how long it took Mama to figure out who the father of my baby was. But when she did, she rushed to my room, picked up the phone, and called Austin. I didn't know who she was calling until I heard her say, "Robin is pregnant, now what are you going to do?"

She didn't bother to say hello or be cordial toward him like she always was. I'm sure he wasn't expecting to hear that because she repeated what she had just said. Then without any regard for him or what he was saying, she slammed the phone down.

Like clockwork, we heard the garage door opening, which meant my dad was home from work. I felt faint. I was not ready for my daddy to know about this. I didn't have time to dwell on what was happening because Mama told us to clean up our faces and pretend like nothing was wrong. She said, "Don't say a word about your pregnancy to anyone." She wasn't going to tell Daddy about it yet. A few moments later, we heard Daddy stepping into the house.

2

The following week, my mom checked me out of school to take me to the doctor. Mama was mostly quiet on the way there. She made small talk by asking me how things were at school. She asked if I was nervous. Of course, I was nervous. A thousand thoughts were going through my mind. I was doing a lot of praying. I was praying to God that I wasn't pregnant, and the test was wrong.

We arrived at Starkville Women's Clinic in no time. The drive was too fast. I was dreading this office visit, but I knew it had to be done. I slowly got out of the car and walked in behind my mom. When we walked in, I felt out of place. I felt like I didn't belong there. I felt shame.

My mom signed me in, and then we sat down to wait. As I looked around, I saw other pregnant women in the waiting room. I also saw wedding rings on their fingers, which made me feel even worse. They looked happy to be sitting there. One lady was flipping through a parenting magazine. Another lady was reading a book while resting one hand on her rounded belly. Then I spotted another lady in the corner sitting by herself. She didn't look happy. She looked sorrowful and sad. Her clothing was wrinkled; her belly was hanging a bit from under her t-shirt. All I thought was that might be me in a few months; pregnant, sad, and pitiful.

My mom shook my leg, pulling me out of my melancholy. I was distracted; I didn't hear my name called. The nurse took me into a small room while my mom took a seat in a chair in the corner. The nurse took my blood pressure, pulse, and weight. She also drew blood for lab work. Next, she gave me a cup for a urine sample. After I returned with the urine sample, I was led into another room that had a pink table with stirrups. There was a sonogram machine at the foot of the table. On the opposite wall, there was a sink with cotton balls, alcohol, and other medical supplies surrounding it. At the head of the table, there was a small end table with a cute little lamp on top, and a chair next to it. Mom stood next to that chair.

The nurse said to remove my bottoms and gave me a paper gown to cover up myself. She left the room to allow me time to get undressed. I was uncomfortable and scared but having my mom with me put me more at ease. I removed my clothing, sat on the paper-lined table, and waited for the doctor. Mom was still standing and pacing as we waited. Neither of us said anything. I didn't know what she was hoping or praying for, and I didn't ask. I could tell she was nervous though.

Dr. Cobb walked into the room and greeted my mom by name. Apparently, they knew each other. In my mind, that wasn't good. It meant I had brought embarrassment and shame to my mother. Truth be told, she never once said she was ashamed or embarrassed by me getting pregnant. She never made me feel like she was either. I never knew if she was or wasn't. I don't think I ever asked her. The only thing I knew was that she was my mom, and she was there for me.

Dr. Cobb was an older, handsome gentleman with brown eyes and dark brown hair. There was a gentleness about him that put my mind at ease. When he talked to my mom and me, I didn't see any judgment in his eyes. I'm certain that I wasn't the first pregnant teen he'd encountered, and I wouldn't be the last. He was kind.

I was instructed to lie back on the hard table with stirrups. He said to put my feet up in the stirrups and scoot to the end of the table. Afterward, he told me to relax. While my mom held my hand, he put a condom on the probe attached to the sonogram machine, along with some lubricant jelly. Then he inserted the probe into my vagina. I had not been expecting this. It was uncomfortable. He was doing what the doctors call a vaginal sonogram to make sure the embryo was attached to my uterus and not in my fallopian tubes. I was also early in my pregnancy, and vaginal sonograms would show the fetus better than the usual type of sonogram.

A few moments later, we saw this little mass of a human being on the screen. Dr. Cobb said, "Look, Margaret! It has a heartbeat." I looked harder, and there it was. Beating. He turned the volume on, so we could hear it. Dr. Cobb said it looked like I was about six to eight weeks. He printed a couple of pictures and removed the probe. I gave him an estimate of my last period, and he gave me an approximate due date of October 25. He helped me sit up, then said he would return in a few minutes with a nurse for the vaginal exam. It all began to set in that I was pregnant.

Dr. Cobb left the room. Mama looked at me and said with awe, "It has a heartbeat." She smiled at me like she was over the fact that I was an unmarried pregnant teenager. I knew right then Mama was going to be supportive and help me in any way she could. I loved her so much. I had done something I promised my mom I would never do. I promised her that I wouldn't get pregnant before my time, yet I did, and she loved me anyway.

Dr. Cobb returned with a nurse to complete the vaginal exam. That was an uncomfortable experience as well. I didn't know what would occur during a vaginal exam. Later, I asked my mom what he had done. She said he tested me for sexually transmitted diseases and scraped my cervix for cells. Having a sexually transmitted disease had never crossed my mind.

After the doctor completed the exam, he said he'd see me again in four weeks and left the room so that I could dress privately. Mom helped me up. I stood there for a moment, trying to process what was happening to me. I put my clothes on, then my shoes, and I was ready to leave. Mom and I walked to the receptionist, and she scheduled me for my next visit. We would have to do the visits around my mom's work schedule because she designated herself to be the person to make sure I got the care I needed.

When we got back to the car, Mama said she was going to take me back to school. We rode in silence back to West Point. I don't know what was going through her mind, but I was ready to burst. All I could think about was how my life was about to change. What were people going to say? What were my aunts, uncles, and cousins going to say? What would my friends say? What would their parents say? What would my teachers think? What was my daddy going to say? What was he going to do? Telling my daddy about my pregnancy was my biggest fear. I knew he was going to be disappointed in me. I didn't know how he was going to react.

Mom seemed to be calm. Deep down, I knew she was as hurt and disappointed as I was, if not more. I hadn't seen her cry since I took the pregnancy test; it looked to me like she wanted to burst into tears as we were driving down the highway. She held her composure well. Maybe she thought that if I saw her crying, I would cry again, and she didn't want me upset before getting to school. While I peeked at my mom from the corner of my eye, my mind kept going back to Daddy.

I didn't want to tell him. There was no way I could fix my mouth to tell my father I was pregnant and going to have the baby. I remembered once he told my sister and me that if we got pregnant, he would kick us out of the house. One part of me believed there was no way he would do it, but there was another part of me that thought maybe my dad would make me go.

I started staring out of the window to hide my face from my mom. I started tearing up at the thought of my father. I didn't want her to see it. The sound of the radio filled the car with tunes from an old school radio station. My thoughts were scattered. My future was hanging in the balance of my twisted life. I was afraid of what tomorrow would bring.

When I returned to school that day, I wanted to talk to Lillie or Shanda about it, but I couldn't bring myself to say anything. I went to each class, pretending like everything was all right. I could hardly focus that day. I was relieved when I finally made it through the last class. It was hard trying to hide my emotions all day. At least when I got home, I could cry, scream, shout, or kick privately. My sister and I got on the school bus together for the ride home. After we got off the bus, we started walking. Dionne asked, "So what did the doctor say?"

I replied, "He confirmed my pregnancy."

She was supportive and said, "It's going to be all right."

We walked the rest of the way home in silence. When we got up close to the house, we noticed that daddy was home. We looked at each other but didn't say anything. Once we got inside, we said, "Hello, Daddy," and went to our rooms. It was awkward; it was only a matter of time before Mama would tell Daddy about the baby. There was no way I was going to be able to do it. We went about our daily activities as usual until Mama got home that evening.

After Mama got home, Dionne and I went into her room, as usual, to sit and talk to her. By the time she got there, Daddy was already outside with his dogs and feeding them and doing whatever else he normally did. Daddy was rarely inside the house when he was home. He'd only come inside to take a nap, and he rarely did that. Daddy loved the outdoors.

"Did you tell your friends that you are pregnant?" Mama asked.

"No, ma'am, I didn't say anything about it."

"Not even to Shanda?"

"No, ma'am." Mama knew Shanda was the closest friend I had. At that time, we didn't talk much because she started hanging out more with some of her other friends. So, that situation only left me with Lillie. Lillie and I became friends in eighth grade when we had a health class together. I wasn't ready to talk to Lillie about it either. There was not one person I knew who would be able to relate and go through this with me. My only hope was that Austin would take care of his responsibility, that we would get back together, and get married.

We had often talked about our future together after high

school. I was going to college to become a doctor, and he was going to the U.S. Navy. Other than Austin, I didn't know if I could share my feelings with anyone. I tried to push those thoughts aside, so I could enjoy the company of my mama before going to bed.

I still hadn't talked to Austin since I'd found out about my pregnancy because he broke up with me. But then he came to me at school and said he wanted to make things work between us. Austin said he didn't want me to have an abortion. I told him I wasn't going to do that anyway. I showed him the sonogram pictures Dr. Cobb printed out as we walked down the hall. He was walking with me to band just as he'd done before the breakup. It seemed like things were going to work out for us, after all. I was willing to try, and so was he. Well, that same afternoon, after I got home from school, I received a phone call from the women's clinic. The nurse called to give me the results of the STD test. She informed me that I had chlamydia, a curable sexually transmitted disease. She said my partner and I would have to be treated, and she'd call in my prescription to the pharmacy with enough medication for both of us.

I hung up the phone in tears and called my mama at work. I was furious and disgusted. Austin had lied by saying he was a virgin. He kept a secret from me, and I was ready to destroy him. I was so upset. I was crying on the phone, telling Mama everything the nurse had said. Mama was able to soothe my spirit; she explained there was no way he could have known he had it because he wouldn't have had symptoms. As far as the lies he told me, there was no excuse.

I didn't talk to Austin that night on the phone. I waited until I saw him at school to tell him about the disease, partly because I wanted to see the look on his face when I told him. When I saw him,

I revealed what the nurse said during our phone call. He blankly looked at me and said, "I'm sorry." I was still upset, but I didn't want to make a scene. I was keeping mental notes on him, and that was strike one. I said I'd give him the medicine once I picked up my prescription from the pharmacy.

A few days later, Mama told Tyra to come to the house to take me to apply for Medicaid after school. As I was about to walk out of the door, Mama said she would tell Daddy about my pregnancy while I was away. However, she did not wait until I left the property; she waited until I got into Tyra's car.

Once I got into the car, I happened to look out the window to my right while I was putting on my seatbelt. I saw my dad crying, more like sobbing, into his hands. Mom was rubbing his back with tears flowing. They were sitting inside his tan pick-up truck parked in front of the garage door.

I saw how much I had hurt him. I couldn't bear to look at him anymore. Mama saw me staring at them and waved her other hand for us to go on. Tyra cranked the car and backed out of parking pad so we could leave. My eyes watered; I tried to blink back the tears, but they slowly fell anyway. I was quiet on the ride to the public aid office.

When we got there, my sister told me where to go to sign in. After sitting for a while with Tyra in silence, the receptionist called my name to go to the back. I nervously stood, walked to the door, and entered a different area of the building. I was escorted to the office of the lady who would be working my case. She didn't even look up at me when I walked in to sit down. She was looking at her computer like she was preoccupied and had better things to do than help me.

Resilient

I sat down in the seat in front of her desk as I waited for her to acknowledge me. She finally looked up and asked, "How can I help you?"

I replied, "I want to apply for Medicaid." She smacked her lips covered in red lipstick and opened her desk drawer to obtain some paperwork.

She went down the page, asking me questions about my life ranging from my age and date of birth down to my expected due date for the baby. I wasn't even sure how to answer some of the questions she was asking me. So, after answering questions about my demographics, I stated I was pregnant, living with my parents, and their insurance would not cover prenatal care for my unborn child and me.

The way the social worker was talking to me added to my shame. There was disdain in her voice as she asked and probed into my personal life. I knew then it wouldn't be long before it was all over town that I'd be having a baby. West Point is a small town; it doesn't take long for gossip to spread. I could imagine people around town gossiping about it. The fact that I knew who my social worker was didn't help ease my concern.

After about fifteen or twenty minutes in her office, she said I would receive a letter of approval or denial in the mail, and then I was dismissed. I still had questions about how long it would take, or what I could I do if I wasn't approved, but I was too afraid to ask them. I walked out of the office, feeling even more disconcerting about my situation. If I wasn't approved, would my parents help take care of me and cover the expenses?

Tyra made me feel a little bit better because she was sure I would be approved for Medicaid without any problems. She said since I was underage and pregnant with no job, the state would approve me. Her assuredness still didn't keep me from feeling like a burden to my parents or society for that matter. When I got in the car to go home, my mind went back to my daddy. I still wasn't sure how he would react when he saw me.

When I got home, I asked Mama what Dad said about the pregnancy. She was quiet for a moment like she was thinking about what she should say. Then she said, "He wanted to know how you could take the word of a boy over his." I didn't know what to say to that. Sure, my dad talked to us about boys here and there, but not really. Mom was the go-to person with our problems with school, boys, and life, in general. Mom should have been the one saying how could I take the word of a boy over hers. She was the one who constantly talked to us about sex and dating.

Daddy remained outside for the rest of the evening in his shop out back. I heard him come in long after we had gone to bed, but long before I fell asleep. I cried myself to sleep that night. I still didn't know what to expect from my father. When I got up the next morning, I got dressed for school as usual. I went and kissed my parents' goodbye as usual, but I got no response from him. Mom said, "Have a great day at school."

Then Sunday came. We got dressed for church and left home. I still hadn't told my friends, so I wasn't concerned about too much gossip yet. Although by the end of service, I knew the news had spread. While waiting in the car with Dionne for Mama to come out, I looked out of the backseat window; I saw her hugging Mrs. Nelson, a lady on the mother's board. She had tears in her eyes after their embrace. I knew then that members of our church knew.

During church, I sat by Shannon, one of my friends from

school. I'd been friends with her since fifth grade. She was one of those friends always making jokes and making fun of other people. When church was almost over, I whispered to her that I was pregnant. I regretted it as soon as the words came out of my mouth. I just wanted to get it off my chest, I guess. Instead of telling someone I knew would keep my secret for a while, I told her. She was shocked, of course, and thought I was lying, but I told her it was true. I told her not to tell anyone. She said she wouldn't; although deep down, I wasn't sure she would keep her word.

The cat was finally out of the bag. When I saw my mom's face as she walked to the car, I wished I could take it all back. Mama walked to the car in tears with her head held down and got inside. She didn't say anything, and neither did we. She fastened her seatbelt, put the key in the ignition, bowed her head one more time, then we left, and headed home.

Mom took Dionne and me skating that night in Columbus. Every Sunday, the skating rink had a skate party called, Soul Sunday. Mom would take us each Sunday that we wanted to go have some fun. We got inside and walked over to some of the girls we knew from school. I wasn't greeted with, "Hello." I was greeted with, "I heard you're pregnant."

Just like that, it had spread like wildfire. I wanted to kick myself for opening my mouth, but I was the one who put it out there for the whole town to know when I told Shannon at church. But, hey, we live, and we learn. I learned who I could trust and whom I couldn't. I learned who I could depend on when I was at my lowest.

I didn't deny it. There was no point in it. Then the girl said, "That's what you get for being fast. Now you got a baby."

I wanted to slap her. She was passing judgment on me like

she was so innocent. She was having more sex than I was; she just didn't have a baby to show for it. I didn't bother to respond to her snide comment. I just walked away.

With the news about my pregnancy going around, I finally told Lillie and Shanda about it. They didn't make me feel bad about it. Instead, they encouraged me and said everything would be all right. I was relieved they didn't say anything negative to me. I was already emotional and feeling bad about my choices and myself. My sister, Dionne, said something to me that I'll never forget when I was upset about what people were saying about me. She said, "You're not the first, and you won't be the last. Don't worry about what they say." I wasn't in the best place emotionally or spiritually, but Dionne's word resonated with me. I thought about what she said, and I decided that I would have to give zero fucks about what others thought of me if I was going to survive my pregnancy. It was easier said than done, but after a while, I was able to do just that.

***

I was glad about Austin and me giving our relationship another chance because I wanted us to be a family. I didn't want to go through my pregnancy or raise our child alone. I knew he wasn't ready to be a father; I also wasn't ready to be a mother. What choice did I have but to go through it? I was afraid for my future, and I needed someone I could depend on. He looked at the sonogram pictures with pride when I showed them to him before, but I couldn't help but feel that this was going to be temporary. It was almost as if God didn't want me to get comfortable with the thought of Austin being around because I was never at ease when I thought of a future with him.

As time passed on, the teachers even discussed my situation amongst themselves. I saw the disappointment and disapproval in some of their faces when I walked into class every day. My mom's friend, Maggie, who knew everybody's business, told my mom she heard about a couple of teachers talking about me in the teacher's lounge one day at school. Austin told me that another teacher pulled him aside in the hallway one day and told him that he had ruined my life.

In May, right before the school year was over, my English teacher, Mrs. Jenkins, read my journal entries regarding my pregnancy. She wrote a snide comment in my journal about me being pregnant. I don't exactly remember what it said, but I do remember how it made me feel. It made me want to cry right there in class. I shed a tear and quickly wiped it away before anyone saw me.

I was ecstatic that the close of the school year was approaching. I could get away from the teachers, students, and their glaring. Little did I know, I would receive the same level of ridicule from some of my church family. Up until my pregnancy, I loved going to our church. Those same people I grew up to love and respect made me feel dejected. It hurt. It hurt me a lot. How could they judge me and count me out? How could they say my life would come to nothing?

3

At the beginning of the summer of 1998, things were looking up for Austin and me. We were talking on the phone just about every day, and he would come by the house to see me. I even went over to his house and talked to his mom, Sharon. Then somewhere along the way, things changed again. He started acting like he didn't want to be bothered with me.

I had an ex-boyfriend, Trey, who called me a couple of times over the summer to check on me. He wanted to give our relationship another try. I told him I was pregnant. He couldn't believe it. I'm sure he already knew about my pregnancy; he probably just wanted to hear it from me. Mom had forbidden me to date this guy. He was a couple of years older than me and lived in Starkville. He was sweet; he never bugged me about sex like Austin did. He knew I wasn't ready, so all we did was kiss and talk. I felt comfortable with him and liked him a lot. Mom made me end it as soon as she found out his age. She felt like Austin was a better match for me.

When I was talking to Trey on the phone, he said I would have never gotten pregnant if I had stayed in the relationship with him. He was right. I more than likely would have still been a virgin. Talking with my ex was comforting to me during the hard time I was going through with Austin. We only talked on the phone a few times during that summer. He wanted to see me, but I didn't feel like it would be appropriate. I didn't want him to see me in the state I was in. My body was changing so fast that I didn't feel comfortable in my own skin.

Austin didn't come by to visit as often as I liked, I assumed he was trying to avoid my daddy. Hell, I even tried to avoid my daddy. When he was home, I mostly stayed in my room. He still wasn't talking to me, and I couldn't take being in the same room with him feeling the disregard he had for me. He could barely stand to look at me. That was a lot to deal with. My little fifteen-year-old heart couldn't handle it. My daddy was my world, and he withdrew from me after I made a mistake. I didn't want to get pregnant. It just happened. I was hurting. I was angry. I was dealing with too much, and I did not have a way out of my turmoil.

Austin's visits didn't make me feel any better. Most of the time, he didn't know what to say to me. He would come over, and we would sit in silence. I was agitated with him. He wasn't at a loss for words when he was trying to get in my panties or when he saw the sonogram. Maybe it was all sinking in that we were having a baby, and he didn't know how to handle it. I don't know what his thoughts were because he never shared his feelings with me. He was silent on the phone and in person. It infuriated me to no end. I didn't bother to share what I was going through with him. I felt there was nothing he could say to ease my pain. I didn't want to continue with our relationship. It was evident we had reached an impasse, and we had no future together. My only hope was that he would help me take care of our baby, and he would be a part of its life.

By mid-July, I was ready to dissolve my relationship with Austin. He was lazy. Yes, he had a job, but every time I talked to him, he was either about to go to sleep or just waking up. He put on a lot of weight. It wasn't the weight that bothered me, though. It was his nonchalant attitude about life I couldn't understand. He seemed to be unbothered regarding our current predicament. That bothered me. It made me uneasy. I didn't want to be with anyone like that. How could he not care about anything? I could not grasp that concept.

I remember calling Austin one day to ask him to bring me something to eat because my mom was at work. I didn't want anything in the house. I wanted some french fries. He brought them over from a fast-food restaurant. I graciously accepted the food, but then he wanted to have sex. I wasn't in the mood for any of that; after all, that's how I got pregnant. I had no desire for sex for a long time. He got upset, and his mood instantly changed.

That was another thing that rubbed me the wrong way. Just because I was having Austin's baby didn't mean he got to have his way with me whenever and however he wanted. I began to accept what we had was over. When he hardly ever bothered to call and check in on the baby and me, I knew then what kind of father he was going to be. It wasn't long before Lillie told me that she saw Austin at his friend, Gary's house. She was hanging out with her cousin, Cara, who didn't live too far from his friend. Apparently, they had a bunch of girls over, and Austin was with one of them. Only God knew what they were doing, but I had a pretty good idea about what was happening there. I knew then and there that things were over between us. After I had time to calm down, I called him. He didn't answer, which added fuel to the fire. He called me back later that day. I told him what Lillie had told me. He denied everything. He said he was there, but he wasn't doing anything. However, I didn't believe him. I wanted to believe him; I just couldn't. My heart was broken again. I was at home pregnant with his baby while he was out with some random chicks having a good ole time. I was pissed! I couldn't get over what Lillie had told me.

We never officially ended our relationship. We eventually talked less and less. We saw less and less of each other until communication ended altogether. I didn't call Austin, and he didn't call me. The last time we spoke, he said, "If you need me, call me."

So, instead of focusing on him and what he was doing, I decided to try to focus more on my future and my baby. I started thinking of names for the baby. I didn't know if I was going to have a boy or a girl, but I had decided on Caleb for a boy, and Ariel for a girl. I watched *The Little Mermaid* every morning during the summer and loved Ariel. She was a mischievous, outgoing, fun little mermaid who loved life. I wanted my daughter to be curious, ready to learn, and love life like that. I looked up the meaning of the name before I was certain I would use it. Ariel is a Hebrew name for males and females, which means "lion of God" or "celestial." When I read the meaning, I knew that was what I was going to name my daughter. Mom likes to think she came up with the name, but she didn't. I knew long before she thought of it, that I would name my daughter Ariel.

I chose Caleb for a boy because my mom said my daddy

wanted to name me Caleb if I had been a boy. So, I looked it up. Caleb means "dog." I still liked the name because Caleb was a spy for Moses in the Bible. Caleb was the one who was confident and loyal; he reported to Moses that they could overtake the Promise Land. I needed a son who would have faith like that. I also felt boys, in general, have a sense of love and protection for their mothers. If I was having a boy, I knew he would be the one man in my life who would love me
.

***

I dreaded going to each doctor's visit. My baby was growing, and my stomach was starting to show. I felt like I was being judged for being an unwed teen mother every time I stepped in the doctor's office. Seeing all of the married pregnant women didn't make me feel any better. I never put my hand on my belly to touch my baby while at the doctor's office; I didn't want anyone to think I was proud to be pregnant. I was still very disappointed in myself and was having a hard time accepting my pregnancy. I woke up every day hoping it was all a bad dream, but in reality, I was only months away from giving birth. During one of my office visits, I found out I was having a baby girl. I wanted a son, but God saw fit to give me a daughter. I didn't mind; I just wanted my baby to be happy, healthy and beautiful.

Although I wanted to be in my room depressed and loathing all summer, my mom wouldn't let me. On the days she was off work, she would get me up early in the morning and take me to the park for a walk. It helped my mood a lot. She would try to get me to talk about my feelings to see where my mind was. Sometimes I thought about opening up, but I mostly kept my thoughts to myself. I wanted to tell her how I felt my brother and sisters wanted me to fail. That might be extreme, but I remember some of the nasty things they said to me that hurt my feelings. It only made me feel more alone and more of an outcast in my family than a member. Although I hid my pain, I came to cherish those walks and the time I spent with my mom. There's no way I could ever repay her for the love and support she gave me during one of the toughest times of my life.

Spending time with my mom during the summer months also helped me get through the rejection I was feeling from my dad. I don't think he purposely kept me at arm's length. I think he didn't know how to cope with the fact that his baby was going to have a baby. When he wasn't working, he was either outside or in his office. When we passed each other in the house, he could barely look at me. It was a painful thing to bear, especially since he had been the king of my life and first love. I felt like he was ashamed of me because people were whispering about me around town. I was too hurt to be angry with him; however, I was bitterly disappointed.

Never in a million years did I think my father would treat me that way. I assumed it was because he was angry, and he didn't know how to deal with that anger, so he didn't talk to me. My dad didn't say much to me. He would say, "Good morning," when I said, "Good morning, Daddy." He would say, "Good night," when I said, "Good night, Daddy."

I wanted so badly for him to hug me and tell me everything was going to be all right. I longed to hear him say, "I love you," or "I forgive you." I had just about gotten over and accepted the fact I was going to have a baby, but I could not get over the rejection from my father.

I remember, early one Saturday morning, I think, my mom was tired of the distance between my dad and me. I was in the bathroom with her while she was putting on make-up; my dad was in the bedroom, sitting in his maroon armchair. I can't remember exactly why, but my mom made me sit on my daddy's lap like I did before I got pregnant. I remember being upset about it because Daddy's face was frowned and hard; he clearly did not want to be bothered with me. I sat on his lap as far away from his chest as I could. When he didn't pull me into an embrace, I started to cry. I sat there crying on his lap, and he just ignored me as if I wasn't there. Mom was trying to get both of us to hug the other, but neither of us would budge. He was stubborn; so was I. I could only give back to him what he was willing to give to me.

Then she got her camera and took a picture of us. She said, "One day, you are going see this and remember how silly you all are acting." After a couple of minutes, I got up from his lap and went into my bedroom with my feelings hurt, with the pain and heartbreak worsening by the minute. I was hurt to the core, and it took me years to recover.

***

When I found out I was having a girl, I started praying for her (which was the only thing I prayed about), singing to her, and talking to her every day. It became more and more real to me that I was about to be a mother, and more apparent to me that Austin was not going to be an active father. I don't think he didn't want to be a part of our daughter's life; I think he didn't know how to be a part of her life. He was probably just as afraid as I was, but instead of talking to me about it and trying to go through it together, he shut me out and stayed away. I didn't understand how he could walk around like he didn't have a care in the world. He could do whatever he wanted whenever he wanted. I was left holding the bag doing everything and going through everything without the one person I thought, despite what I was told, would stick around.

I turned sixteen in July of 1998. I want to say I had a happy "Sweet 16" birthday party, but I can't. Mom, however, surprised me with a cake and told me about the baby bonds she had been buying at the hospital. She bought them so I could have a nice room during labor and delivery. I was on Mississippi Medicaid. She said those rooms weren't the best in the hospital. She would know because she worked there. Mom wanted me to be comfortable. I thought that was the sweetest thing. During the early part of my pregnancy, I felt nobody cared about my feelings, but my mom came through like she always did. She touched my heart and my life in ways she can't even imagine, and I will love her forever for that.

I also received some baby girl's clothing. Although they were hand-me-downs, they were nice. I was given a tote filled with beautiful dresses, bloomers, socks, and booties. I knew Ariel would get to wear them, and she would look so cute. Austin's mom already loved her unborn granddaughter and made sure I got them. I'm not sure who they came from; I was just grateful. That was one less thing for my mom and I to worry about.

4

I returned to school in August with a big, round belly. I didn't want my mom to bother with buying maternity clothes, so I wore a big t-shirt to cover my jeans. I wore my pants unbuttoned and unzipped, held up with a belt I found in my mom's closet. The ensemble was a little uncomfortable some days, but it worked.

I fell into the swing of things easily. I went to class with my head held high. I was determined to prove to my teachers and myself that I could maintain my excellent attitude toward my education. I was unwavering when it came down to my grades. My friends didn't treat me any differently, and I had their support. I don't know what was said behind my back, but none of them made me feel bad to my face.

They would ask me questions like, "Are you happy about the baby? Are you excited?" I didn't even know how to answer those questions. I was scared out of my mind, so how could I be happy or excited? All I felt was terror. I couldn't honestly answer their questions with a yes. But I did say yes because what kind of soon-to-be mother wouldn't be happy about having a baby? Well, I knew what kind; I just couldn't tell them that.

I shunned away from school activities. I didn't want to go to any football games during the months leading up to my delivery. Before it was time to vote for Junior Maids during homecoming week, I was asked by some of my classmates if I wanted the votes. I didn't want the votes because I didn't feel beautiful anymore. I felt fat, ugly, and ashamed. I was disgraced with myself, and I could not stand the thought of what I had done to my life. During my sophomore year, I was elected to be one of the Sophomore Maids for my class. I guess some of my classmates assumed I wanted to be one of the maids again. I did not want to be a pregnant spectacle on the football field. Nor did I want to bring anymore embarrassment to my family. The worst part about my shame was that my relationship with Austin was over; I don't think either of us knew how to make things right. We were much too young to be going through so many changes. We didn't know how to communicate effectively with each other, which was another sign that we were not ready to be parents.

A few weeks after school started, my daddy had a talk with me about my upcoming responsibilities. To my dismay, he decided to have this "talk" on a Friday night while my friends were out at the football game and going to parties, while I was at home alone. Coincidentally, it was also the same night Austin was out having a good ole time with friends. Daddy asked me, "Where do you think that boy is going to be while you are at home with a pot belly? Where do you think he is going to be while you are at home rocking that baby?"

I was so angry with him for asking these questions, and in my anger with a nasty attitude, I said, "He's going to be right here with me." Deep down inside, I knew I wasn't speaking truthfully, but I didn't want my daddy to know he was right.

Then Daddy said, "No, he's not. He's going to be running the street, living his life while you put yours on hold." I was hurt and furious with my dad. It felt like he was rubbing my misdeed in my face; he was adding insult to injury. I wanted Austin to prove him wrong. As much as I hated to admit it, I knew my father was speaking the truth. After that dreaded conversation, I went to my room to lay in my bed, and I cried until I drifted off to sleep.

Tay, one of my friends, came up with an idea during our math class. She asked me if I was having a baby shower. I told her no. She said, "You should have a baby shower. I'll give you one. You can have it at my house!"

I was pleasantly surprised. I didn't think any of my friends' parents would let them host a baby shower for me, let alone at their homes. It brought joy to my heart that she made such a sweet gesture. Right then and there, she and Nikki, another friend of mine, planned my baby shower. In class of all places! Nikki said she would bring the cake. Tay said she would decorate and provide the food. She made out a list of all my other friends to invite.

The day of my baby shower, I was still in shock. I couldn't believe it was happening. It was a beautiful sunny day. The weather was nice. I felt great! I felt better that day than I had felt in a long time. Tay's parents made me feel welcome in their home. My friends were there, and they brought plenty of gifts for Ariel. I was excited and thankful. I don't think I stopped smiling for a minute. Mom didn't go, but she was just as elated as I was. Dionne went with me.

From what I saw, she was having a good time as well.

After the shower, we got everything home, and I started putting things away. It suddenly occurred to me that in less than a month, I was going to be a mother. Reality set in, and so did the anxiety and frustration once again. I tried to shake it off and enjoy the moment, but I couldn't. I was too angry at God to even pray about it. That is a terrible thing to say, but those were my feelings.

I was angry He let the devil get me pregnant when there were so many other girls at school having way more sex than I was, and they were baby free. I was angry that I had listened to Austin and ruined my life. I was angry at Dionne because her life was still normal, and mine was screwed up. I was angry at my daddy for turning his back on me. I was sort of angry with my mama for meddling and practically forcing me to date Austin. I felt like if she had let me date the other guy I was interested in, I wouldn't have gotten pregnant. I was angry with everyone. I blamed everyone but myself. I didn't want to take responsibility for any of it.

It was all too much. I was trying to be happy, but I had so many raw emotions. Those were emotions I didn't know how to deal with, so all I could feel was hurt and anger. I did not want to face my truth, but it was my life. It was a life I was not ready to live. It was the freedom I was not ready to give up. It was hope I did not want to see fading, but it was fading every day. It was difficult putting on a smile every day for others to see because when I was alone with myself, I hated what had become of me. I felt like my life was hell, but I couldn't tell a soul, not even my mama.

A longing for love, acceptance, and validation started right there. I didn't think anyone could or would accept me the way I was. So, not even knowing it, I started to change. Long gone was the sweet girl who loved life and everything about it. What fell upon me was a spirit of self-loathing and insufficiency. Maybe all the people who said I was going to be nothing now that I had a baby was right. I started to feel like I was never good enough, and I would never be good enough. The sad part was that there was not one person in my life who would understand it.

To prepare for Ariel's arrival, I washed all of her clothes with *Dreft*, a liquid detergent specifically for babies. I also boiled her bottles, nipples, and pacifiers so she wouldn't get thrush. I prepared her crib with the bedding Mama bought from Wal-Mart. It was a *Precious Moments* bedding set that I fell in love with while we were shopping. We also purchased Vaseline, A&D ointment, baby powder, and diapers. While I was in the kitchen boiling the water to sterilize Ariel's bottles, Mama looked at me and said, "You're going to be a great mom, Robin." I'm glad she thought so. It gave my confidence level a small boost because she saw something in me that I didn't see.

Preparing for parenthood was an emotional experience for me. I cried a lot and hid the unrest I was feeling from everyone as best as I could. I cried once at church, but Mom didn't seem too pleased with that. So, I buried my feelings inside as deep as I could and put a lock on them. I refused to let them out. Whenever I was asked how I was doing, I said, "Fine." Whenever someone asked me if I needed anything, I said, "No." That is how the last few weeks of my pregnancy went.

Resilient

October 10, 1998

Dear Journal,

I'm ready to have my baby! I'm tired of being pregnant. I'm ready to see her. I cried at school the other day after my doctor's appointment because he said I hadn't dilated at all. My back hurts. My feet are swelling. I'm tired of looking like a sack of russet potatoes. God, please let her be beautiful, healthy, and look like me. Oh, yeah, I hate my life!

5

On the morning of October 18, I started having pain in my lower back. I told Mama my back was hurting, and the pain wouldn't stop. It would come and go. She started getting excited. Mom said, "I think you're in labor! Get dressed so that I can take you to the hospital."

I didn't think I was in labor, but I did as instructed. When we got to the hospital, the nurses put a monitor on my stomach, took my blood pressure, and started an IV for some fluids. Mama had a feeling they were going to send me home, so when the nurses left the room, she told me to start crying so they would keep me.

I said, "Really, Mom?"

She said, "Yes! I'm ready to see my grandbaby!" Her excitement had doubled between the ride to the hospital and the starting of the IVs. Oh, yeah, my mom had to start my IV because my veins were too small; the nurse, who introduced herself as Sara had to stick me twice.

When Sara came back, on cue, I started crying. It wasn't hard to do. All I had to do was think about how my life had been turned upside down. Because my mom worked at the hospital and knew everyone so well, they all agreed I should be admitted. I spent the night in the hospital. Mom was there with me all night. I found it hard to sleep because I was anxious about what would occur the next day. That night of all nights, I prayed. I knew I hadn't talked to God much, but that night, I asked Him to protect Ariel and me during childbirth. I asked Him to let me live through it and to keep the angels with us. I drifted off to sleep shortly after my prayer.

The next morning, I was awakened by my new nurse, Katie, bright and early. A nurse came in from time to time through the night to check my blood pressure, but it didn't bother me too much. I was bothered, however, the following morning because I wasn't ready to get up or give birth. Katie brought in a bag and hung it on the IV pole next to my fluids. I didn't know it at the time, but it was oxytocin, a drug used to move labor along a lot quicker than it may otherwise go. Mama was smiling; she had her camera taking pictures. Mom was on cloud nine. She was ecstatic that I was going to have my baby that day.

Katie asked me shortly after my drip started if I wanted an epidural. Before I could even answer, my mama said, "No! She will not be having one of those today." I was going to say no anyway because I'm afraid of needles. Then Mama went on to say, "You're going to feel all that pain, baby, so you won't have to go through this again."

I tried to hide my sarcasm when I said, "Yes, ma'am," but I didn't hide it well because I rolled my eyes, too. After Katie left the room, I turned on the television to have noise in the room. I wasn't really watching it. I was looking at it, not paying attention to what was on.

Mama started making phone calls. She called Sharon, Austin's mom, and told her I was in the hospital and going to have the baby that day. Then she called Uncle Charlie and Aunt Elizabeth and told them. She called Daddy last. She wanted to know if he would be coming up to the hospital to see me. I'm not sure what he said, but he didn't show up at all that day or any other day.

When she got off the phone with him, she looked disappointed. Mama tried to save face and smiled at me. She said to relax. I wanted to cry, but I didn't. I tried to let it roll off my back and not let it get to me. He had been so cold during my pregnancy. So, I wasn't surprised he wasn't coming.

About an hour-and-a-half into the drip, I started having painful cramps. The nurse gave me some pain medication through my IV. It relaxed me a lot. I still felt the pain, but it took the edge off. Austin and Sharon came to the hospital right when the pain was starting to kick in. Austin sat in a chair across from me so that every time I looked up, I was looking directly at him. He looked like he was worried. Mom was amused. Every time I moaned in pain, he tensed up and looked like he wanted to pass out. Sharon and Mama grinned each time. Mama kept picking at him, asking if he was all right. He would nod his head, although I could tell he was scared to death. He didn't try to hold my hand or anything because we had barely spoken in the months leading up to my labor.

He probably didn't know what to say or do. He looked like he wanted to sit next to me. On the other hand, I saw fear. He didn't know how I would react, so he may have thought it was best to stay where he was. Honestly, I wanted him to try to comfort me, but he didn't. I had become so numb over the past couple of months that it didn't bother me too much. I'd almost accepted the fact I would be doing this on my own, but I still wanted him to step up. I still wanted him to show some interest in wanting to at least try, yet he didn't.

Katie came in and out, checking on us as the morning went on. At some point, she said she was going to break my water. I was confused but said okay. She explained what she was going to do. She used a tool that I didn't see to pop the sac. It was kind of gross because water drained all over the pad I was lying on. She wanted to see if Ariel had had a bowel movement during labor, and indeed she had. There was brown stuff in the water, and I was horrified. *This is gross!* Katie and Mama helped me sit up; the pad on the bed needed to be changed. It was just my luck to start having a contraction while all of this took place.

Between 11:00 and noon, the contractions started getting closer and closer. I thought I would not be able to bear it. I told Mama, and she asked Katie if I could have some more pain medication. Before she could answer, Katie said she had to check to see how far I had dilated. Well, the good news was I was progressing wonderfully. The bad news was it was too late to have any more pain medication. *This is fucking great!* Not only did I have to go through the rest of the labor feeling every cramp and every bit of pain, but I also would not have one drop of medicine to take the edge off.

Mama came and stood on my left side while Sharon stood on the right. Mama was telling me to relax and breathe. Sharon was rubbing my back, rocking me a little, and saying, "It's going to be okay." She was starting to annoy me! I did not want to be touched! I wanted to tell her to get her hands off of me and let me be! Only I couldn't do that without being disrespectful and hurting her feelings. I just had to bear it. Austin was still sitting in the chair, but this time, he was slumped over with his head in his hands.

The worse the pain got, the more afraid he became. He finally got up and walked out of the room. Sharon looked at the door and walked out behind him. Mama stayed with me for a few minutes. When they did not come right back into the room, she left to see what was going on. I assumed Austin went out into the hall and had a panic attack or something. To this day, I still don't know what went on after he left the room.

A moment later, Mama came back and took her place next to the bed. Every time I felt the pain, Mama automatically knew it; she said, "Relax and breathe." She showed me how to breathe slowly and deeply, so I wouldn't panic; I watched her and mimicked her breathing pattern.

Katie came back in to see how far along I was. I had dilated to nine centimeters. Mama got excited and said, "It's almost time!" She started giddily clapping her hands. Mama was ready. Katie said, "It won't be long now, Margaret!" I saw the excitement in Katie's eyes.

Sharon returned just as the nurse was walking out. I'm not sure if Austin was with her. I was consumed with pain; I didn't take the time to notice if he was there or not. Sharon returned to her place on my right side. Mama got her camera out and started snapping more photos. Sharon was smiling. She was just as excited as Mama and ready to see Ariel. I was the only one in the room terrified. A little after one o'clock that afternoon, I felt the urge to push.

Mama left the room to get Katie and told her I had to push. Katie ran in and checked me. She said, "Oh, yeah, Margaret! It's time! I paged Dr. Pearson when she was nine centimeters to let him know to get ready."

"Where is Dr. Cobb?" I asked

"It's the weekend baby. Dr. Pearson is on call this weekend. I promise you, he will take care of you too," said Katie.

Then she firmly said, "Do not push! Even if your body is telling you to, do not push!" In a matter of what seemed like seconds, Katie had adjusted my bed to let the stirrups up, Sharon and Mama had gowned up, and there were maybe three other people in the room already gowned up. *I'm really about to have a baby!* It all happened fast; I don't even remember seeing them all walk in. I was focused on not pushing; I missed all of it.

Dr. Pearson walked in with his hands up, palms toward his face. The nurses immediately opened his gown for him to walk into. While one nurse was donning his gown, the other nurse was donning his gloves for him. I was amazed at how they did that so gracefully. I'm not quite sure how he got the hairnet on because I had a contraction and focused on not pushing. He looked at me and said, "All right, don't push until I tell you to." He stood back, looking down at my vagina. I'm sure he was gauging how my body was reacting. I noticed scissors in his hand, but I didn't know he had used them until after labor was over.

He sat down on his stool and said, "Push!" I was pushing but wasn't doing it correctly because my bottom started coming off of the table. Katie yelled, "Stop!"

I stopped. She said, "Bear down like you're having a bowel movement."

I looked at Mama. Mama held my hand, and said, "Breathe, Robin, you can do this. Just try to relax. You have to breathe." I

Resilient

remember my eyes got watery, but I didn't let the tears fall. She said, "Look at me!" I looked at her.

Mama started taking deep breaths and told me to do what she was doing. I kept looking at her and breathing like her. I was in sync with her. I was able to tune everyone else out. I forgot the pain for a moment to be in sync with my mama. It was a beautiful thing. Then she said, "Now push." She heard the doctors when I didn't.

I turned back to face Dr. Pearson, and I bear down to push like Katie had told me to. Then, I stopped for a moment to catch my breath. Then Dr. Pearson gave me the go-ahead to push again. I pushed, and boom! Just like that, Ariel popped out. She came out so fast, Dr. Pearson had to jump back a little to catch her. It was something I wasn't expecting. He said, "Wow! It's a girl!"

After clipping her cord, he gave her to the nurses. I assumed the nurses were from the neonatal unit the newborn babies go to. They placed her on the baby's table. There was a heater above the bed, and it was on. When the nurse put her down, Ariel started rolling from side to side, screaming her little head off. She was having a newborn baby fit. I didn't know babies could roll around like that so soon after birth. One of the nurses called out, "Time of birth; 13:35." I heard another nurse say, "Oh, my God, I've never seen a baby do this before."

Mama said, "Oh, my Lord, look at her!" She was anxious to hold Ariel. Once she was calmed, the nurses wiped Ariel down and put ointment on her eyes. They put a cap on her head and bundled her up.

While the nurses were working with her, Dr. Pearson was working on me. It wasn't long before my placenta and remaining tissue delivered on its own. When all it fell down into the bag placed at the foot of the bed between my legs, it was the best feeling in the world. I felt ten pounds lighter. Dr. Pearson started sewing me up. He'd done an episiotomy; I didn't even know he had cut me. My vaginal opening started to tear, so he cut me to prevent further damage. While Dr. Pearson was working on me, Katie gave Ariel to Mama. Mama cried as she held her and told Ariel how beautiful she was. Mama held Ariel down a little for me to see her beautiful face. I remember saying, "She looks just like Sharon," then my head flopped back. I closed my eyes. I was exhausted.

When Dr. Pearson finished stitching me up, he touched my arm. I opened my eyes, and he said, "Congratulations, Robin. You have a beautiful baby."

I smiled and said, "Thank you."

"I'll be back tomorrow to check on you!"

Then he left the room. I looked around, and everyone had cleared the room. They had cleaned up and removed any evidence of me giving birth a few moments ago. I looked to my left, and there my mama was holding Ariel. She smiled at me; then placed Ariel in my arms. I looked down at her lovely round face and smiled. I couldn't stop smiling or feeling all the love I was feeling at that moment. I couldn't take my eyes off of her. "Hello Ariel, I've been waiting to meet you."

I noticed her head was shaped funny. It was cone-shaped just like those aliens in the movie *Coneheads*. I asked Mama why her head looked like that. She said, "Oh, she is fine. We just have to shape her head." I had no idea what she was talking about, but Mama took her from me and started molding Ariel's head in her hands like it was a ball of clay. I thought maybe it would hurt, but Ariel didn't cry or anything. Her eyes were closed. She looked peaceful.

Resilient

Afterward, Mama gave Ariel to Sharon. Sharon grinned from ear to ear. She was happy to finally hold her granddaughter. She said, "Hey, Pooh-Pooh!" Hence, Ariel had a new nickname from her grandma. From then on, every time her dad's family saw her, they called her, "Pooh-Pooh." I don't remember when Austin came back into the room; I looked up, and he was there. His mother put Ariel in his arms, and he looked scared to death. He probably thought he was going to break her because I thought I was going to break her, too. I was afraid to even put her Onesie on.

One of the nurses from the nursery came in after about thirty minutes to take Ariel to the nursery. It was time for her to be thoroughly examined and given a bath. I was hesitant to let her go, but Mama assured me she would be fine. I noticed a monitor had been placed on Ariel's foot, and we were given matching bands (one for her foot, and one for my wrist). That made me feel confident she wouldn't be stolen from the hospital. I know it may seem silly to worry about that, but I had heard about babies being kidnapped or mixed up at birth.

The nurse asked me if I was going to breastfeed the baby. I was going to say yes because I'd read it creates a bonding relationship with the baby but again, my mom jumped in and said no before I could answer. *Well, damn! I can't even breastfeed my baby?!*

When the nurse left the room, my mom told me to put my bra on. She tightened it so much I thought she was going to cut off my circulation. She said I shouldn't breastfeed because I was young, and my breast shouldn't sag.

Mom and Sharon talked for a few more minutes; then Sharon and Austin left. As he was leaving, we looked at each other without saying a word. Just before he walked out of the door, he looked back and said, "I'll see you later."

So that's it? Still no plans for us? Don't you want to stick around to see the baby when she comes back? What the hell?

I said, "Bye."

Mama didn't say anything. She raised from her chair and stood next to the bed. She gently touched my face just above my left eyebrow to move a strand of hair out of the way. She looked at me and said, "It's going to be all right." It was like she could read my mind. She was always telling me everything would be all right. I wanted to believe her, but I didn't see how my life could get any better. All I saw was darkness.

After giving birth to Ariel, I was waiting for my dad to come, only he never came. I know Mama called and told him I had the baby. I asked her if my dad was going to come. She said she talked to him, but he was working. In the back of my mind, I knew it was because he was ashamed of me. I knew he wasn't going to come even when he left work. Once again, my feelings were hurt. I felt even lower than I did before knowing my father didn't want to have anything to do with me.

I was allowed to walk the halls of the hospital. I had some pain, but my mom was there to help me walk it out. I thought she would have to work, but she took some days off to be with me. She was by my side the entire time. She slept at the hospital with me; she made everything better. When the nurse would bring Ariel to me, Mama taught me how to put the diaper on correctly. She taught me how to hold Ariel while she was feeding. She encouraged me while dressing her. Mom said, "You won't break her." I was hesitant to lift her arm to put clothes on. Mom taught me the correct way to snuggle Ariel and how to lay her down when it was time for her to sleep. She said, "Don't hold her too much, you don't want her to be spoiled."

After a couple of days in the hospital, Ariel and I were ready to go home. Dr. Shirley, a pediatrician from the local pediatrics' office, came in to see me the day after Ariel was born. She said Ariel was a healthy and happy baby girl with no problems. That was music to my ears. Having a healthy baby was an answer to my prayers for her. My doctor made his rounds at the hospital the day before we were discharged. He wanted to make sure I was feeling well enough to go home, and that I had a bowel movement before leaving. He gave a prescription for pain and a stool softener. Because I had an episiotomy, he didn't want me to strain with any bowel movements. Another tear would slow the healing process. I was also given a disposable over-the-toilet perineal sitz bath kit to aid the healing process.

I was terrified of leaving the hospital! My mom would be there to help me, but I was still afraid. Ariel was so beautiful, and I didn't want to hurt her. I didn't know the first thing about taking care of a baby, but I was sure to learn quickly. As we were leaving, my mom's friends, who worked at the hospital with her, bid us a farewell and congratulations. The male transporter helped me get in a wheelchair and rolled me out of the hospital to the car. Ariel was already buckled in her car seat. Mom had to bring it in before they would let us leave the hospital. It was a little windy outside; Mama covered Ariel's face with a blanket. She said, "I don't want her to get colicky."

I had no idea what she was talking about, but I said, "Okay." Mama put Ariel in the car first; then she helped me get into the car.

I moved slowly to keep from hurting myself.

Before I got into the car, I looked up at the sky, as I often did as a child, and I still do to this day. It was a beautiful day. It was cool and partly cloudy, but still gorgeous. All I could do was smile. It's something about looking up that always brightens my day even when there isn't a hint of light in my life. Mom closed the door to her black Mazda 626 and walked around to the driver's side to get in. She started the car, and we headed home.

6

Mama dropped Ariel and me off at home and headed out to go pick up Ariel's formula. I had already been approved for the WIC (Women, Infants, and Children) Program. However, my mom had to take proof of Ariel's birth to the social services office to obtain the voucher for the milk. She left us alone in an empty house. I don't know where my dad was, but I was glad he wasn't there. The silence was comforting.

I carried Ariel to our room. I normally would have gone to my mom's room, but I didn't want to risk being in there when my dad came home. I lay Ariel down on the bed and watched her. She was peacefully sleeping. I couldn't take my eyes off of her. I didn't understand why God had chosen me to give birth to her. I couldn't understand why He allowed it. I still felt like He let the devil ruin my life. I stood there, hoping I wouldn't make an even bigger mess of her life.

Mom returned home a little while later with Ariel's formula.

She was upset with one of the staff members at the social services office. The woman was giving my mother a hard time about the paperwork because it was close to closing time. She didn't want to deal with it and told my mom I had to come back the following business day. My mom was pissed. She came home cursing and calling that woman everything but a child of God.

She carried the formula to the kitchen. It was a powder. This was my first lesson in parenting. I made a mistake and learned from it all in the same day. I wasn't quite sure how to mix the formula. The directions on the container said I could make a pint, but to boil the water first. I boiled the water like I should have, but I didn't wait for it to cool. I put the powder in the water; it clumped together. I felt stupid. How was I going to take of this child if I couldn't even mix the formula right?

I started over. I boiled more water. The second time, I let it cool. After it cooled, I put it in a pitcher because I didn't have a jug. I put the water in the fridge, and I mixed the formula by the bottle from then on. That was something I had to sit down and figure out on my own. Mom said it had been too long for her to remember.

For Ariel's first feeding at home, I quickly learned to warm and test the milk before giving it to her. I held her in my arms while she cooed and whined a bit, then I put the bottle to her mouth. She quickly latched on and began sucking down the milk. It sounded like she was about to choke. It was as if she was drinking too fast. Mama told me to stop feeding her. She assisted me in getting Ariel up, so she could burp. *That was easier than I thought it would be.* I lay her back down in the crest of my elbow and was about to continue feeding her. Mom stopped me again and said to hold her at an angle so her milk could go down easier and reduce the risk of reflux. It worked like a charm.

Later that day, my dad came home. I went into my room with Ariel to avoid him. I heard him go into their bedroom. The door remained open; I heard everything. I left my room and went into their bedroom to say hello to him. He barely spoke back without looking at me. I turned around to go back into my room. Ariel was lying in her crib, placed across from my bed, next to the window. She was sound asleep. I picked her up to feel some comfort. Just smelling her scent and watching her sleep made me understand that I now had a purpose. I had to take care of her.

After a few minutes of silence, I heard my dad talking to Mama. He said, "You need to go tell her to get out."

"Where do you think she's going to live, Robert?"

"She can go live with that boy that knocked her up!"

"I ain't telling her a damn thing," Mama said with malice. "If you want her to go, you go down that hall and tell her."

He didn't say anything. Then Mama went on her rant. I remember it like it happened yesterday.

She said, "You're sitting up here acting like you are perfect when your ass has done everything under the sun but died. I tell you what! If she goes, then I go, and I ain't going no damn where." Wow!

I was stunned! I sat there on my bed, paralyzed. Mom was awesome! She was my advocate. She refused to let my daddy make me leave home. I don't think I had ever been so grateful to have her than at that moment. Without her, I don't know what would have become of me. I shudder to think about what my life would have been like if my mom had not stood up for me. She loved Ariel and me. She wasn't going to let my dad ruin me. But little did she know,

I heard everything, and I was already ruined. While I was grateful for her, I was displeased with my father. I couldn't believe he thought so little of his child that he would want to throw his grandchild and me out on the street. There was no way in hell I was going to live with Austin and Sharon, whether my mom had been there to save me or not. I would have gone to a shelter first!

I heard my mom coming down the hall to my room. She walked in and saw me sitting there, holding Ariel. She said, "Give me this baby." I held her tighter because I didn't want her to take Ariel away from me. She looked at me and said, "Give her to me." Mom didn't yell, but her voice was stern. I loosened my grip. She gently took Ariel from my arms, left my room, and went back to her room.

I heard Mom say, "Take this, baby!" I knew she had put Ariel in my dad's arms. Then she said, "Just look at you; you ought to be ashamed of yourself! That's right! You should be crying, sitting up in here acting a fool!"

I was shocked at the way my mom was putting my dad in his place. I had never heard her speak to him that way. I couldn't hear his response; I didn't hear him say anything. Perhaps his demeanor was just a façade to keep me from seeing how he really felt. It was hard to tell. He never told me how he felt about me getting pregnant and having a baby. I assumed he was ashamed of me. I knew I had embarrassed and deeply hurt him because before the day my mom told my dad I was pregnant, I had never seen him cry. So, I knew he was hurting. I was hurting as well; we couldn't figure out a way to effectively communicate our feelings to each other. I still loved him very much; I don't believe there was anything I could have said or done to make him understand how sorry I was for hurting him.

Resilient

From the moment my dad found out I was pregnant, our relationship morphed into something I didn't recognize, nor could I understand. For a fifteen-year-old girl whose dad had been her world, that was difficult. I had no words to describe the pain I was feeling. I still don't have those words today. It was a pain my mom couldn't fix. It was hurt I felt that God couldn't touch. It ran so deep some days I wanted to die. Sometimes I would lay in my bed and cry at night not knowing what to do or who I could talk to. I had no one. Mom didn't like to see signs of weakness. My friends at school wouldn't understand. My sisters had their own lives to live. So, I did the only thing I could. I buried my feelings deep inside and tried to be strong. I had no other choice.

I went back to school two weeks after giving birth. I wasn't ready to leave Ariel, but I was getting depressed sitting at home every day. Mama had gone to the school to get my assignments, but I wanted more classwork to do. Ariel slept most of the day, and all I did was watch television once I finished my assignments from school. I also missed my friends. Lillie and Shanda came by the house to see Ariel after she was born, but that was the only interaction I had with my friends after I'd given birth. I dropped Ariel off every morning with Austin's mom because she wasn't old enough to go to daycare yet. Sharon was helpful. She loved Ariel very much; she took excellent care of her until she was old enough to go to daycare. She gave unwanted advice, and so did my mom, but I knew their intentions were good. It was all part of having a child at such an early age.

My grades at school were still great. To keep from thinking about how I messed things up at home, I focused on school. I went to school and pretended everything was fine as usual. A couple of weeks after I returned to school, Mr. Dorroh, my Advanced Placement Biology teacher, sent a letter to my parents:

November 10, 1998

John Dorroh
C/O West Point HS
P.O. Box 616
West Point, MS 39773

Dear Robin and Mr. and Mrs. Terry:

I just wanted to take a few minutes to tell you how much I appreciate your concerns over not getting behind in Anatomy & Physiology in your absence, Robin. Not only did she keep up with her work, Mrs. Terry, but she participated in a presentation the day she returned to class! So many times, students use the excuse that they were absent to not do their work.

I think that too much time is spent concentrating on the negative behaviors of just a few students. It's time that good students, conscientious students receive some credit, too. Robin, I am very proud of you for making sure that you did not get behind in your work. You wrote in one of your journal entries how you wanted to go to medical school. This sort of perseverance is what it will take, and you certainly can do it!

Mrs. Terry, it was so good to see you here in your daughter's absence to collect Robin's work and make sure that she did not fall behind. I wish more parents were like you.

Please call on me in the future, Robin, when you need a reference.

Resilient

Sincerely,

John Dorroh, WPHS

I was flabbergasted! I could not fathom why he took the time to tell me he was proud of me, but I'm glad he did. That letter encouraged me and gave me another push. I needed to not only graduate from high school, but to go to college and pursue an actual career. He believed in me, and that meant something to me.

When I saw Mr. Dorroh, I wanted to express my gratitude with many words, but all I could say was, "Thank you." I wanted to hug him and say how much it meant to me, but I refrained from doing that. I didn't know if it would be appropriate or not.

As he said, "You're welcome," I saw sincerity and pride in his eyes. I knew I was a student he was proud of.

7

When Ariel was about eight weeks old, I got a job at Sunflower, one of the grocery stores in town. I was hired the same day I went in to inquire about an opening. The job came right on time. I made minimum wage, and it was enough to pay for daycare. Daycare at the time was $50 per week. My entire check went toward daycare and putting gas in my car. I had an old, manual 5-speed car Mama made Daddy give to me to drive. Whatever, I couldn't cover for Ariel, my mom took care of. Mama was willing to help me as long as I was trying to help myself. Austin didn't give me a dime to cover childcare, formula, diapers, or clothing. I didn't like working at Sunflower. As always, I did what I had to do. I was always working on the weekends. I probably worked three out of four Sundays a month. I was disgruntled and bitter about it, but I needed the job. I vividly remember the Sunday of Ariel's christening. I had to work, and I was disappointed I couldn't be there. Mom and

Sharon took it upon themselves to take care of it. I was Ariel's mother, and I should have been there! I wanted to be there, but as usual, they took over. I cried that day. I was irritated my entire shift at work. Mom was oblivious to my feelings.

I was grateful for the support of my mom. She stood up for me and cared at the most vulnerable time of my life. So, how could I tell her I was angry? How could I tell her I felt she excluded me out of one of the most important days of my daughter's life? She probably didn't see anything wrong with it because she and Sharon were loving grandparents.

It wasn't just the christening that had me upset. Mom and Sharon were always trying to tell me what to do. I know some girls my age, who got pregnant, didn't have that kind of support, but at times, it was overbearing. I wanted to pierce Ariel's ears, but my mother said no. I wanted to paint her nails sometimes when she was a toddler, but my mother said no. Sharon tried to tell me how to comb her hair, what diapers she should wear, what diaper ointment to use, and so on. It was driving me nuts! Ariel was my daughter, but the grandmothers were treating her like she was their daughter. I appreciated the advice but hated it at the same time. I was only sixteen; I didn't want to appear to be disrespectful or ungrateful. So, I kept my mouth shut and nodded my head to keep down confusion.

Being a new mother, working, and going to school was a challenge. It was hard, but not so hard that I felt stressed out all of the time. I was able to juggle my responsibilities just fine. What I couldn't handle was the pain and rejection buried inside of me. I also had some resentment toward Austin and unforgiveness toward my father. My thoughts often wandered back to that Friday night, and how my life could've or would've been different. I wouldn't be using my entire paycheck to pay for childcare. I wouldn't have disappointed my father so much he couldn't stand the sight of me. I wouldn't feel rejected by Dad or my child's father. I wouldn't have been afraid of what the future held. If I had just gone with my first thought and said no, my life would've been a lot easier. I wouldn't have any troubles. Don't get me wrong; I loved my daughter. I just wasn't ready for all that came along with her. I constantly had to hide the fears and contempt I felt for myself. I didn't even like to look at myself in the mirror.

When Ariel was an infant, I'd pray and cry often. I was praying God would rescue me. I was hoping my life was a dream, and I would wake up at any moment and be back to normal. I had to deal with my reality, with what was real and happening in my life. I didn't want to face it. It wasn't until I matured in Christ that I figured out the repercussions of the decisions made whether good or bad, must run its course. My life was running its course based on the decision I had made that Friday night. It was my own doing. As difficult as it was, I had to accept that.

Ariel was a beauty. I had to figure out a way to come to terms with the fact that I was her mother. I was the one who decided to have sex, and now I had to deal with the result of my decision. I came to the realization that I couldn't blame anyone but myself. I wanted to blame my mom, but I couldn't. She'd told me long ago to wait to have sex, and if I felt I couldn't wait to come to her, so she could help me. I wanted to blame my dad, but I couldn't. He never really talked about boys, but I knew he wouldn't approve of his little girl having sex, especially at fifteen. I wanted to blame Dionne, but my big sister told me to use a condom if I was going to do it. I wanted to blame Austin, but he didn't make me do it. Yes, he coerced me, but the ultimate decision was mine. I had a voice, but I didn't use it. Why? I wanted to fit in. I wanted Austin to like me. I was curious. I wanted to know what all the fuss was about when it came to sex. *Well, believe me, it's certainly overrated.*

It wasn't long after Ariel was born that Austin's stepfather got a promotion or new job in the Carolinas somewhere. I think it was sometime after Christmas, early 1999. Austin could have remained in West Point to live with his grandmother, but he chose to move away with his mom and the rest of his family. He had lived with his grandmother on and off for years. He'd leave home and live with her when he couldn't get along with Sharon. So, he could have stayed if he wanted to.

I was foolishly still hoping we would be a family. But when he left, I knew that would never happen. He already wasn't taking care of his responsibilities to his daughter. As if that wasn't enough, he put hundreds of miles of distance between himself and us. I mean, damn! Was it that hard for him? No, it was hard for me! He had disappointed me and let me down. There was no coming back from that. Right after Ariel was born, I tried putting him on child support. I had to open a case for her to get Medicaid anyways. Unfortunately, because he was a minor, he could not be forced to pay it. My caseworker told me she could only award me $25 a month. Really? Twenty-five dollars wouldn't even cover a box of diapers or daycare. Unfortunately, I never got that $25. He never offered me a dime. He came to visit her now and then. I never wanted to keep him away from her. It wasn't my place to do that even though I was infuriated with him. She had a right to know who her father was, and he had a right to see her. I didn't want her to grow up and say, "I don't have a relationship with my father because my mom kept us apart." Every child should have the opportunity to know and spend time with his or her father as long as he is not a threat to the child (even if he doesn't do his part financially). A child will eventually grow up and figure his or her dad out for themselves.

    I digressed. Austin moved away. He never called or sent her anything. She was only an infant; she didn't know any different. I didn't know how long he would be gone or if he was ever going to return. He could have left out of fear, or he could have left because he didn't want to try to be a father. I don't know. He didn't tell me why he was leaving; I didn't ask. I cried then, too. I pretended like I didn't care, but it hurt me. I was hoping Austin would prove my father wrong and be there for us; but again, he did not. Everything my father said while I was pregnant was true. He told me Austin would leave me and live his own life. He told me Austin would let me carry the burden of parenting Ariel on my own. I didn't want to believe my dad because everything he was saying was hurting me, yet it all turned out to be true.

    Although I was dealing with the residue of a failed relationship twice over, I had to press on. I didn't let it keep me from trying to move forward. Little did Austin know that when he moved away, some of the boys at school, who didn't say two words to me while he was there, all of a sudden came out of nowhere trying to date me. A couple of them probably liked me for who I was, and the others liked me for what they wanted. I could tell the difference. One of Austin's good friends, Nathan, tried to date me. He said he wanted to help me take care of Ariel, and Austin was a fool for leaving. Can anyone say shocked? I couldn't believe it! Where was his loyalty to his friend? He was breaking cardinal rule number one. As flattered as I was, and as trifling as I wanted to be, I said no. It wouldn't have been right. As much as I wanted Ariel to have a father in her life, it couldn't be him. He was persistent for a couple of weeks. He stopped by my house a couple of times after school, but I wouldn't open the door. I parked on the back, hoping he wouldn't see my car, but he knew I was there. He eventually dropped it and moved on. I was relieved when he did.

8

During the summer of 1999, I'd had as much as I could take. I was tired of dealing with my feelings on my own. My daddy was still halfway talking to me, although he doted on Ariel every chance that he got. He loved her, and I'm so glad that he did. I knew somewhere in that heart of his that he loved me too. I just wished he would show it sometimes. I never understood why he could display his love and affection for her, but he couldn't do the same for me. I don't think he understood how bad that made me feel.

I was also still angry with Austin for not being there and helping take care of his daughter. I thought of him often, and I couldn't stand it. I wanted him as far away from my mind as possible, yet he crossed it almost every day. What caused me even more anguish was the fact that I wasn't sure he was even thinking of Ariel or me. It had been months since he'd left. I still couldn't seem to move past the thought of him not wanting me or loving me like he said he would. How could he walk away so easily? Once again, the words of my father came to my remembrance. I remembered everything negative my dad had said. It burned me up to know my dad called it before I could give birth. It's funny how we can always remember the negative over the positive. It's easy for negativity to creep in. Focusing on the positive is the hard part.

I started secretly drinking and smoking to numb my pain. We all know we must be eighteen years old to buy cigars and cigarettes, and twenty-one to drink alcohol in this country, but not a soul ever carded me when I went to buy Black & Mild cigars or alcoholic beverages. I loved the sweet smell of Black & Mild, and inhaling the scent made me feel like a different person. I smoked in the car whenever Ariel wasn't around because I didn't want her inhaling the smoke. I kept my lighter in my purse and hid the cigars in my car to make sure my mom didn't find them. I drank Fuzzy Navel's alcoholic beverages. They weren't strong, but it was enough to calm my nerves as often as I needed it to when I was filled with self-hate, loathing what my life had become.

I resented Austin for what he had done to me. It appeared to me that he didn't have a care in the world. If he did, he never showed it. One particular evening, I was irritated. I didn't want to be bothered with anyone. For once, I just wanted to be a free-spirited teenager again. I wanted that more than anything in the world. I wanted my life to go back to the way it was. It was about seven or eight o'clock at night. I was desperate to leave the house. I asked my mom if I could go out. She started asking me a thousand and one questions. All I wanted was a yes or no answer. I vividly remember what happened that evening. I had a nasty attitude with her. I think she wanted to hit me, but she didn't. She asked, "What is wrong with you, Robin?"

I didn't say anything. I looked to the floor, trying to find the words to express what I was feeling. She said, "Answer me!"

I looked at Mom and said, "I don't want her anymore!"

I couldn't believe that came out of my mouth. It wasn't that I didn't want Ariel anymore, I didn't want the life I had anymore. I wanted to die. Mama looked at me in disbelief. She probably didn't even know how to respond to what I said.

"Get out of here. Go on and leave."

I did exactly that. I got my keys and left home. I didn't know where I was going. I drove around and decided to call one of my guy friends. He was home, but his parents were not. He told me I could come over and hang out with him for a while. Deep down, I didn't want to be there. I did, however, need to feel wanted by somebody. I needed comfort, and any comfort he could offer would do. He wasn't a stranger. I knew whatever happened between us would stay that way. That was the first time I had been with someone since I found out I was pregnant. It didn't make me feel any better; I only felt worse. Somewhere in that agony, I felt like I deserved it. I'd screwed everything up a long time ago.

I should have run to Jesus with my pain, but I wasn't interested in talking to Him about it. My mindset then was that God let the devil get me pregnant. God let the devil ruin my life. I felt that perhaps God had no interest in me. Let everybody else tell it, I was going to hell anyway. My life was forever messed up. Besides, I didn't think God cared much about my pain when there were other people in the world with problems bigger than mine. One of the few times I consulted God, my question was, "Why am I the one who got pregnant? Why am I suffering when I'd only had sex one time and got pregnant? I just wanted to see what sex was like, and I got pregnant the first time! Really, God? Why me? Why did you let the devil do this to me?" I waited and waited for an explanation because there was no logical explanation to me. I barely spoke to the Lord unless I was crying and questioning why everything had turned out badly for me. I was somewhere I never thought I'd be. I thought He had left me.

It wasn't long after I lashed out that Ariel got sick. She was eleven months old with a horrible cough. The sound of it made me cringe. She was cranky and cried a little bit after each cough. I knew it had to be hurting her. I took her to the pediatric office in West Point. The doctor listened to her chest and prescribed an antibiotic.

I'd given it to her for a couple of days, but her cough and breathing only seemed to get worse. Mom came home from work and held Ariel. She listened to her chest with her stethoscope and said, "Something is not right." She asked, "Do you think we should take her to the hospital?" I was terrified; she was struggling to breathe. Every time she inhaled, her chest and stomach went tight enough to show her rib cage. Her respirations were deep and slow like she was gasping for air. The wheezing was loud.

I said, "I guess so; she looks like she can't breathe."

"Good answer," Mama said. "Let's go."

Instead of going to the hospital in West Point, Mama drove us to Starkville to the emergency room where she worked. We didn't wait to check-in. Mama scanned her badge, and we walked directly to the back. Mama found an empty room and said, "Stay here with Ariel."

The room was cold, and the lights were bright. I sat Ariel on the bed and stood in front of her to make sure she wouldn't fall. She was still struggling to breathe, yet she sucked on her pacifier like

Resilient

she didn't have a care in the world.

In no time, my mom walked back into the room with Dr. Henry, an older gentleman with brown eyes and dark brown hair. He wore his glasses on the tip of his nose which showed his age. He spoke to me, then turned his attention to Ariel. He placed his stethoscope on Ariel's chest. He said to undress her. I took her clothing off as quickly and gently as I could. He put the stethoscope on her back and listened to her breathing again. Then, he laid her back on the bed and listened to her again. A nurse who introduced herself as Jessica, came into the room. She had a small pulse oximeter. She placed it on Ariel's little finger and waited. I couldn't read the number from where I was standing; I had stepped back so she and the doctor could continue their examination.

Nobody said anything to me; the doctor looked at my mom, and said, "Okay, Margaret, let's step into the hallway."

Mom, Jessica, and the doctor left the room. As they left her bedside, I walked back over to Ariel, trying to figure out what in the world was going on. Ariel's chest was still heaving, and with each breath she took, she struggled to inhale. A few minutes later, a sweet and funny respiratory therapist came into the room to give her a breathing treatment. She put the mask over Ariel's nose and mouth. Ariel was just about to start fussing when the respiratory therapist started singing to her. She sang a goofy song about elephants or something. It was a tune I had never heard before. Ariel stopped fussing and started listening.

Oh, great! She just needed a breathing treatment. Everything is fine. We'll be going home in no time. Or so I thought.

After about a minute or two, the respiratory therapist started hitting Ariel's back. It wasn't a painful hit, but it was firm. She kept singing to her while she was doing it, and it didn't seem to bother Ariel. I looked at her with a disgruntled face, wondering why the heck she was hitting my baby in the back. She saw my expression and stopped singing about elephants and started singing to me in the same tune, "It's okay, Mom. I have to loosen the phlegm, and this helps." I nodded my head, indicating I understood. Then she continued singing to Ariel.

When the breathing treatment was over, Ariel got sleepy and started falling asleep. I held her in my arms, ready to get her home, so we could both go to bed. We were tired. Mom came back into the room. This time, the pediatrician on call, Dr. Lott, came in with her. I assumed he was about to tell us that we could go home. Instead, he said he was admitting Ariel into the hospital. "I'm glad you brought her in because she wouldn't have made it through the night. Her oxygen level is extremely low. We're going to have to put her in an oxygen tent. The next couple of days are critical." If I hadn't been sitting down holding my baby, I would have passed out. *What the hell?!* He just told me my baby could have died!

When the doctor left the room, I started crying. It had suddenly hit me that my life wouldn't be the same without her in it. I loved her so much, but I spent all that time wishing she had come along later rather than sooner. I spent all that time hating what my life had become. Now, I might be losing her. Mom hugged me. As she rubbed my back, she said everything was going to be fine. I felt terrible because not too long ago, I didn't want any part of the life I had. But if I had lost her, my life would never be the same.

Earnestine, my mom's friend, who was a paramedic at the hospital, came in to check on us. After chatting for a few minutes, she and my mom left the room to talk some more. I still had Austin's phone number; I decided to call him. I thought he might want to know his daughter was in the hospital. The phone rang. Just when I was about to hang up, he picked up.

"Hello."

"Hey, Austin. I was calling to tell you Ariel is sick, and she is being admitted to the hospital." I held the phone waiting for him to say something.

"Okay."

Okay? Is that all you have to say? No questions about what's wrong? Do you even care how she is doing? I wanted to yell at him and curse his ass out, but I didn't. I felt rejected and alone all over again.

"All right, then." I slammed the phone down. *Maybe he really doesn't give a damn about her.* Words could not express how angry I was with him. When he should have been there with me caring for his daughter, he was off in La-La Land. *Wow! I am really in this alone.*

Just like clockwork, my mom walked into the room and asked if I called Austin. I shared exactly what had happened. She said, "I'll talk to Sharon later."

It wasn't long before an orderly came to the emergency room to escort us to Ariel's new room. The room was small and quaint. It was clean and cold. There was a crib the size of a twin bed off to the left side of the room with a clear tent over it. The bed had rails on all four sides of it. The rail closest to the wall was up, but the other side was down. A chair was adjacent to the bed, and there was a bluish-green sofa against the other wall. The fluorescent lights were bright white and clashed with the checkerboard linoleum on the floor. I looked to the left and saw a small sink area with a low light above it. I knew that was the light I would have on in the room. It was just right, not too bright, but not too low. Above the bed, there was a large canopy, called an oxygen tent, big enough to cover from the head to the foot of the bed and side to side. I couldn't tell where the oxygen was entering the canopy, but I knew somehow it would be there. Ariel was still struggling to breathe. Although the amount of exertion it took her to inhale had decreased a little bit, I could still see and hear the difficulty.

Ariel's nurse for the night came into the room shortly after we arrived. She introduced herself as Kelly and wrote it on a board on the wall. Kelly had to be in her early twenties. She had a bubbly personality with her small five-foot frame. She said it would be perfectly fine to lay in the bed with Ariel as she slept. Kelly gave me a small gown, big enough for a toddler, to dress Ariel in. After she left the room, I removed Ariel's clothing and kissed her forehead. I dressed her in the gown, then held her close to my heart. For the first time in a long while, I took the time to whisper a prayer, "God, it's me, Robin. If you're listening, please save my sweet baby. Don't let her die. Don't take her away from me." As I walked to-and-fro, I gently bounced her in my arms to soothe her. Ariel fell asleep, but I continued to hold her. I didn't want to put her down.

Kelly and my mom came back into the room. Mom told me she was going to head home. I wanted her to stay with us at the hospital, but she assured me we would be fine without her. "I'll come by first thing in the morning to bring some clothes for you to go to school." Mom said with a kiss on my cheek and kiss for Ariel. Kelly told me to lay Ariel in the bed under the tent. I did as I was told. I stood by the bed. She said, "Go on and climb in."

Before I got in, I took off my tennis shoes. I didn't have any pajamas to put on, so I got in bed with my clothes on to lay to the right of Ariel.

Once I was in, Kelly let the rail up, and said, "If you need to get out, push the nurse's button on the side of the bed." She zipped the tent, and as she exited the room, she turned off the fluorescent light. The sound coming from the tent was serene. Ariel was sleeping peacefully. As much as I wanted to stay awake and watch her all night to make sure she didn't stop breathing, I couldn't. I turned on my left side and cradled her as I drifted off to sleep.

Ariel was in the hospital for a week. I left her every morning in the care of the nurses so that I could go to school. As soon as I got out of class, if I didn't have to run home for more clothes, I went straight to the hospital. By day five, she was her usual self again. She was standing in her crib, holding on to the rails talking, jumping, and playing. I was elated to see her active again because while she was sick, she barely moved.

She was discharged on a Friday afternoon. The doctor said to buy a cool-mist humidifier and turn it on every night at bedtime. I followed those instructions. She slept under a humidifier through the rest of the fall and the winter months. I was thankful she was still with me. I thanked God for not taking her away. *Sometimes it takes almost losing your loved one to know how much you love and need them.* I knew that day I would never take having Ariel in my life for granted again. She was my sunshine. She was the joy of my life, and I was so happy that God allowed her to see her first birthday.

Resilient

9

My senior year of high school was an emotionally trying time. I had a newfound love for my daughter that I didn't have before, yet I couldn't stand the thought of her father. I still longed for love and affection from my father. I still didn't know what would become of my future. I hoped I would get a scholarship to college, but I didn't know where to start. I'd succeeded at everything I thought to put my mind to. I got a job. I was still on the honor roll. I had been inducted into the National Honor Society. I had been elected a senior maid on the homecoming court. I'd been in a pageant. I was a cheerleader. On the outside, all appeared well with my soul. To look at me, you'd think I had it all together. But I was dying inside.

I thought about killing myself most days of the week. I thought of driving my car into a ditch a few times. I thought about driving off an overpass and crashing my car. Leaving my house, there was a stop sign at Old Tibbee Road and Section Road. Directly in front of that stop sign was an open area filled with trees, and only God knows how deep the fall is. Many days, I sat at that stop sign and contemplated driving into it, hoping I would die. If I drove fast enough and went through the stop sign, I could end it all. I wouldn't have to worry about anything. My parents would take care of Ariel, and I would be done with this life of rejection, emptiness, and pain.

One day, I was sitting at that stop sign thinking about what I was going to do, and a voice came to me. It said, "Your life is not yours to take." I sat there, trying to figure out if I'd heard what I thought I'd heard. I was thinking, *Surely God was not speaking to me*. I did not drive off the road that day. I thought if that was God speaking to me, then maybe I should give life more time. Things might just turn around for me.

My senior year of high school, Austin moved back home. Things went from bad to worse. He'd been home for a while and not so much as seen or asked about Ariel. On top of that, a rumor started that he was dating my best friend, Shanda. I was in the school's choir. I heard about it at choir practice from a friend of mine. I didn't believe it for a minute, but I wanted to break off in his ass about something. I didn't care what it was. So, I used that rumor as a means to tell his ass off. I did it the next morning in the school's cafeteria. I never intended to say anything to Shanda about it. I didn't believe she was dating him, but a mutual friend of ours overheard what I was saying to Austin, and she blew it up.

I told Austin he was a sorry excuse for a father and needed to help take care of our daughter. I was doing everything alone (with the help of my parents, of course). Every week, my entire paycheck went to daycare, diapers, and baby food, or whatever else I could afford to pay for. I was angry and hurt that he didn't take the time

Resilient

or initiative to be in her life.

It was a huge mess. Shanda walked in and sat at our usual table as Shannon started blabbing about how we've been friends too long to let some boy come between us. Shanda had no idea what was going on. I didn't get a chance to explain it. She got offensive, and I did the same. Lillie came in to sit down, but by the time she got there, everything was in disarray. She whispered to me not to say anything to Shanda about the rumor, but it was too late, Shannon had already spilled the beans.

The bell rang, indicating it was time to head to class. Austin was pissed off and started following me. He was trying to talk, but I ignored him and went to my locker to get my things for class. By this time, there was a crowd of students following us, trying to see what was going on. He was cursing and talking to me at the same time. I couldn't hear what he was saying. All I saw was red. I was furious and wanted to turn around and punch him in the face. My fury wasn't about Shanda and whether or not they were dating, it was about his lack of concern for his child.

He walked up to my locker, asking me what my problem was. I screamed, "Get the fuck out of my face!" Then I slammed my locker and headed to my first class of the day. It didn't help matters that Shanda and I had just about every class together, and she would be in class with me. The moment I stepped foot into my class, I heard a commotion coming from the hallway like students were yelling or something. *What the hell is going on?* It was probably nothing, so I just went to my seat. I was crying and upset. I did not want to be there or be bothered.

Mr. Dorroh walked into class. He could see something was seriously going on; I was crying, and so was Shanda. Moments later, my mom walked into class to see me. *What? What is she doing here?* I have no idea who called her, but she took me to the side. She was asking me what was wrong, but I couldn't even answer. I stood there crying. She talked to Shanda as well. She was trying to figure out what was going on, but neither of us said anything.

Mama said, "You girls have been friends since fifth grade. You can work it out. What's wrong?"

I wanted to grab Shanda, hug her, apologize, and tell her she did nothing wrong, but my pride and shame kept me from doing so. I thought she had immediately written me off as a friend. I was angry with life, not with her. Shanda just happened to get caught in the middle. Mom left the school; I stayed there, taking in what had transpired that morning.

It turned out the commotion I heard was Austin and Lillie, fighting in the hallway. I didn't even remember seeing Lillie in the hallway, so I had no idea why it happened. I was informed Austin said, "I don't have time for y'all bitches."

Lillie replied, "Your mama is a bitch." Or something like that. Then he attacked her. I don't know who stopped the fight or why he had the nerve to put his hands on her. His anger was probably more directed toward me, and Lillie got caught in the crossfire just like Shanda. Lillie and Austin were suspended from school. Lillie came back after her suspension, but Austin didn't return. He dropped out of school.

Shanda didn't speak to me for a few days. When I finally got up the nerve to apologize to her, I did. However, our friendship wasn't the same after that. She forgave me, and I'm glad she did, but she kept me at a distance. I can't say I blame her. I hurt her in a way I never thought I could hurt anybody in a million years. She and

Resilient

Lillie got closer. I hung out more with my sister and other friends I grew up with in Dunlap.

All wasn't well. I pretended like it was while still thinking about dying most days. Instead of thinking of ways to kill myself, I waited for death to come. I felt alone more than ever. I knew if something happened to me, my parents would take care of Ariel without question. As I had heard before, my life wasn't mine to take. But it was His to take, and it would have been all right with me if He decided to take me away. Sad to say, but true.

I applied to a few colleges. I couldn't go too far away from home since I had Ariel. I wasn't going to be the mother that left her child with the grandparents for them to raise. Since God had chosen to let me live, and I decided to see how my life was going to turn out, I was determined to be an active mother. I had my mind set on being a mom, a student, and working so I could take care of myself and my daughter. Ultimately, I chose to go to Mississippi University for Women (MUW) because it was close to home. MUW was only about a twenty-minute drive from home. I could live at home with my parents and commute to class easily every day without neglecting my daughter. Before graduation, there was an awards' ceremony at school. I was in the top ten, not ten percent, but number ten out of almost two hundred students, which was another goal of mine. I started out being number seven, but I took Advanced Placement Calculus. It dropped my grade point average a tenth of a point, which booted me to number ten. I knew I would need that class in college, so I took it in high school to get a feel for what the class would be like. Taking that class gave me an advantage in college; I was glad to have taken it.

The local newspaper, The Daily Times Leader, covered the

ceremony and listed our names in the paper along with a photo of us on stage. I was proud of myself. I'd gotten a scholarship to MUW and was well on my way to a brighter future. I saw the paper and gave it to my mom. She hugged me and said, "I'm proud of you." She was in tears and overjoyed.

Then, she passed the newspaper to my dad. I didn't expect anything from him. After all, he'd once told me I was going to be in poverty. When he read it and cried, I was taken aback. I couldn't believe it. The only other time I saw him cry was when he found out I was pregnant. He held his head down almost as if he was ashamed. Dad said, "I'm proud of you," and hugged me. Tears slowly rolled down my face. I had been waiting to hear those words for the longest time. I was inducted into the National Honor Society; he didn't come to any of the ceremonies. He didn't come to the football game during my senior year when I was on homecoming court. He didn't come to the hospital when Ariel was born or when she was sick. He barely spoke to me. All that time, I thought he was ashamed of me. It was like he didn't want to be seen with me in public because of what I'd done. Hearing him say he was proud of me touched my heart, but it did nothing for the pain that was there.

On June 2, 2000, I graduated from West Point High School with honors. It was hot out on that football field, but I was glad to be done with high school. I was ready to leave all the pain and shame behind. I was ready and looking forward to what I was hoping would be a brighter future.

Resilient

July 30, 2000

I'm eighteen years old today. I've overcome a lot. Many said I wouldn't even graduate from high school, but I did it! Many said I was going to be nothing because I had a baby so young, but they are wrong. I am going to be great. I am going to prove all of them wrong. I'm thinking about medical school or pharmacy school. I'm not sure which, but I know whichever way I decide to go, I'm going to be successful. I guess I have a lot to live for. My daughter needs me, and I need her. I can't imagine life without her. She's my sunshine. She gives me a reason to keep going. I want to make her proud. I want her to look at me one day and see strength and success, not failure. If I don't have any other reason to pursue a better future, it is for her. Mom did it, and because my mom did it, I know I can do it.

I think I'll get a tattoo.

God's Glory

Looking back, I've looked for God's glory in my pregnancy and everything I faced until I went to college. Being as young as I was, I felt like God had abandoned me. I was in church my whole life. I was there every Sunday; Sunday school, and all. When I got pregnant and was being talked about by some of the members of the church, it hurt me. They made me feel horrible. I associated the church people with God. If they talked about me and said I had no future, I thought that surely God felt the same way. That's why we have to be careful about how we treat people, especially the young and vulnerable. Those who come hurting and bearing the shame of their mistakes should be loved on, and not judged. It is not our job to judge anyone; to tell them their life is over or that they're going to hell, no matter how we feel or what we think of the choices they have made. It is our job to love one another. God is the judge, not us. A lot of times, Christians are quick to forget we, ourselves, are not perfect. We all make mistakes. God uses our mistakes for our good. According to Romans 8:28, "All things work together for the good of those who love God: those who are called according to His purpose (HCSB)." So, be careful not to be the cause of a soul turning away from Christ due to your self-righteousness.

I digressed. I was so young; I didn't have a personal relationship with God because, during that time, that's not what I was taught. I wasn't taught to be personal or intentional about my faith. I was taught to look a certain way and act a certain way, the do's and don'ts of the Ten Commandments, the Beatitudes, and so on.

I was also hurt by my father, a devout churchgoer, and

deacon. To make matters even worse, I was hurt by Austin. In my dismay, I turned away from God because every example I had of His love had hurt me. Little did I know, hallelujah, God was still there for me. I was able to juggle school, work, and studying because of God. I was able to keep my grades up and remain on the honor roll because of God. I was inducted into the National Honor Society because of God. I received scholarships to college because of God. I had a drive to keep pushing because of God. My daughter survived her sickness and is alive today because of God.

Even though God did all of these things, I barely prayed. I barely acknowledged Him. I was bitter and angry, filled with resentment, and unforgiveness. And I blamed Him for all I felt was wrong in my life. How foolish I was, and I didn't even know it. But God is faithful, and He is merciful. He is forgiving through our foolishness and bad choices. It was God who helped me survive. It was God who kept me alive through that tumultuous time. For that, I am forever grateful.

God's glory, in this part of the story, is that He is always there. I want you to know that He will see you through hardship and difficult times even when you are too foolish to seek Him, know Him, love on Him, acknowledge Him, and thank Him. He will be there, and He will prove Himself to you, for His namesake, just for you. That is what I want you to hold on to. He won't leave you even when you leave Him. He is relentless in His pursuit of you. God loves you!

Resilient through Unwise Choices...

10

I started at MUW and started attending a new church, which I'll discuss later, the fall after I graduated from high school. The campus of MUW was small but beautiful. Some of the buildings were older, but they still held the original character I appreciated. Mature trees and green grass covered most of the campus. It was a new experience. I felt like I was in kindergarten again, trying to make friends. Tay, the friend that hosted my baby shower in high school, also started at the MUW. Aside from her, I didn't know anybody. She lived in the dorms, so she met new people and started friendships quickly. I met a few people through her by eating lunch in the union.

I still felt out of place there. The majority of the girls got to hang out together and have the dorm experience I would never have. I commuted to class every day. I felt like something was missing in my life. I had my health, and my daughter was thriving, but there was a void in me that needed to be filled. I was on speaking terms with God again, so I asked Him to bless me with a friend. A friend who wouldn't hold my past errors in judgment against me. A friend who would be able to walk the walk of faith with me. I needed a confidant. I didn't want to feel alone in the world anymore. I needed someone I could bare my soul to. I also wanted to know more about God and the Bible. I wanted to have a real relationship with Him. I wanted to be an excellent mother. I wanted a father for my daughter. I wanted to be successful. I wanted God to help me!

It turned out that God does answer prayers. I met a few young ladies in college that I got to know, but the friendships didn't grow into the type of friendship I needed. Perhaps it was because I had my guard up. Perhaps it was because I was too afraid to let anyone in on the details of my life and how I was personally struggling. Perhaps it was because God knew exactly what I needed when I needed it, and I wasn't going to get it until He saw fit.

The fall of my freshman year, I met Tameka in one my classes. When I told Tameka I had a daughter, she was thrilled. Ariel started attending the daycare on campus when I started college. I let Tameka meet Ariel one day after class. She instantly fell in love with Ariel. Tameka babysat Ariel when I had to work. I was working as a pharmacy technician at Wal-Mart. I also had a work-study job on campus in the library. Ariel loved being with her. Tameka fed her, bathed her, and played with her without charging me a dime. Talk about divine intervention! She helped me out with Ariel even when my sister wouldn't. It hurt my feelings that Dionne wouldn't keep Ariel sometimes, but I couldn't blame her. She had her own life to live. Tameka was supportive, and I appreciated that about her. I didn't talk to her about my feelings or my life, but we did share mutual respect; I grew to love her as a person. She had such a sweet spirit, and she loved Ariel. To show my appreciation, I wanted to do something nice for her for Christmas that year because she truly was a Godsend. I had gotten a credit card so I could buy clothes for Ariel and myself. I used my credit card to buy her something for Christmas. It wasn't much, but she happily accepted my gift.

During my freshman year of college, I also met April. She would soon become the friend and confidant I had prayed for. When we met, we instantly connected. We met in a class we had together. We talked all the time during class. I swear, I thought we would get kicked out by the professor. I could whisper. April, on the other hand, couldn't whisper if she tried. So, we had to start writing notes like we were in grade school. It's silly, I know, but sometimes class was just boring. We often skipped class to have a long lunch or hang out at the Columbus Lock & Dam, a lock & dam along the Tombigbee River. There was a nice picnic area there. It was a beautiful place to go hang out and enjoy the weather when it wasn't raining or too hot. We talked about everything, but what connected us, in the beginning, was our thirst and hunger for God. I knew there had to be more to God than what I'd seen growing up. I wanted a relationship with Him, but there was still a lot that I didn't know or understand. I was still a babe in the faith, but she was much stronger than I was.

April and I set out on a mission to know and love God more. Over two-and-a-half years, we developed an unbreakable bond. Many days, we found ourselves walking up and down the aisles of Books-A-Million in Columbus, looking for devotions and books to read together. We talked about prayer and fasting, which we also did together. I was able to talk to her about everything going on in my life, and she did the same. We were like two peas in a pod. My faith was strengthened, and I'm sure her faith grew even more. She imparted words of encouragement and tried to make me feel good about myself. It was because of God using her that I began trying to see myself in a different light. Even though I struggled with the need for validation and all of the other emotions I dealt with, her words lifted me.

Over time, and it took a lot of time, not only did I begin to see myself differently, I began to see God differently. It was all about me establishing a relationship with Him. I had a thirst for Him like I never had before. Now I wasn't afraid of God. I had a love for Him that I never had before. I wanted Him to know I loved Him. I couldn't get enough of reading my Bible. I felt good when I read His Word and His promises. Although I had more trials you will read about later in this story, I now had something man couldn't take away from me. I had an actual relationship with my heavenly Father. It made all the difference in my world.

It was through work on my part, wanting and working on my relationship with God, that I was on the path to wholeness. I saw the error of my ways and way of thinking. I began to see I didn't need validation from man, not even my father. God showed me, through His Word, that I had to rid myself of unforgiveness, resentment, and self-loathing. All this did not happen overnight. It was one day at a time, step by step, verse by verse.

While God was (and is) working on me, there was a battle constantly going on between my flesh and spirit, between me wanting to do what I wanted and doing what He wanted. I still made mistakes, a lot of them, but I had to keep trying and keep striving toward righteousness. I'm still doing that today. I'm still not perfect. No one is, so it's important we don't beat ourselves up about what we've done wrong. Even I had to learn to forgive myself after I had forgiven others. Forgiving myself was the hardest thing to do out of everything I was working toward.

In studying the Bible, I came across a verse that says, "It is I who sweep away your transgressions for My own sake and remember your sins no more (Isaiah 43:25, HCSB)". I said that to say if God can forgive us, then we can and should forgive ourselves. If God can forget about it and wipe the slate clean, then we can and should be able to do the same. When the enemy began taunting me with my past transgressions, I could now shut him down with the Word. That's why reading and studying the Bible is important. That's why having a relationship with God is necessary.

***

I digressed. Back to the story at hand.

During the summer of my sophomore year in 2001, I had made plans to move out to get an apartment. It was time to be out on my own with my daughter. I thought I was ready to find my own way in the world. Besides, Ariel needed to understand who her mom was. She had gotten to where she would listen to my mom more than she listened to me. I couldn't have that. I wasn't going to have my child calling me by my first name like I was her sister. Between my two jobs and my refund check, I would be able to pay my rent, utilities, and cell phone bill. I didn't have a car note. Daddy paid for my car insurance. I received assistance with paying for Ariel's childcare, which cut my out-of-pocket costs by more than half. I had it all figured out. I was going to school year-round, so I could hurry up and get done with undergrad, hoping to move away to go to pharmacy school at Ole Miss. I was in a hurry. I wanted to start making more money to take care of Ariel. I know now that no one can rush destiny, but I was trying to. What can I say? I was young and hungry.

When I finally let my mama in on my plan, she cried. I was her last baby at home. She did not want me to move out. I explained to her that I was ready to be on my own and wanted Ariel to know me as her mother and not her. I explained to Mama that it annoyed me for Ariel to listen to her over me. If I told her to do something, I was ignored. But if my mom said the same thing, she would instantly do it. It was clear that she saw my mom as the authoritative figure and not me. It was frustrating; I was ready to go. Mom asked me not to move out, but I said I was going to anyway. Then she said that if I was moving out, she was as well. *Say what now?*

This wasn't supposed to be a joint venture. I intended to do this on my own. However, I couldn't ignore my mom's feelings and the fact that she was about to embark on a new journey of her own.

I agreed to get an apartment with my mom and be her roommate; therefore, I had to put my plans on hold. As soon as Mama found a place for us, she left home. It was official, Mom and Dad were separated. It was hard to witness. I watched my daddy cry just as I had watched my mom cry off and on from time to time through the years. I was hurting for them. I loved my parents. I wanted them to be together, but I also needed both of my parents to be happy. I'd grown up with both of them my whole life, so I knew when there was happiness in the house and when there wasn't. Their separation hurt all of us, but it seemed necessary. I had seen my mom be resilient since I was a little girl; I knew she would be fine. I had seen my dad be a man's man my whole life, but I was praying he would still be all right. Mom had been a constant in his life since before I was born. I had never seen my parents apart. I didn't know how my dad would handle being without my mom. I just prayed that everything would be okay.

11

I still had to eventually get my own place because like I said, Ariel needed to understand who her mom was. Shortly after moving, my mom had newfound independence. She seemed happy and free; it was written all over her face. She started going out more with her friends and was starting to enjoy her life. It was then that I knew it's just not worth it, being unhappy for so long.

During the fall of 2001, I went out with Dionne, to a club right outside of town called Club Excalibur. It was a huge club for our area. Most of the clubs we had gone to in the past were holes in the wall. Excalibur was well-lit, had a lot of floor space, and places to sit around the perimeter of the club. There was also a long bar running along the front wall, where people could stand to buy drinks, although I'm not sure if they were selling alcoholic beverages. I wasn't old enough to purchase a drink, so I didn't bother to find out. I didn't pay much attention to whether or not people were walking around with cocktails or beer. I was more or less trying to have good, clean fun with my sister. It had been a while since we had hung out together.

While sitting in one of the chairs, I spotted a cutie with a couple of his friends. He was at least six-feet tall, light-skinned with a low haircut. He had a slim yet muscular build. He was fine. I didn't walk up to him or anything like that. I wasn't that bold, but I did keep my eyes on him most of the night. I remember watching him as he walked around and danced a little bit. I saw his smile and the spark in his eyes; I loved it. His smile was contagious because every time he smiled, so did I. He hadn't noticed me yet, and I was glad because I was seriously ogling this man. I could not take my eyes off of his face.

While I was preoccupied with this gorgeous creature, it turned out his friend was peeping out my sister. Before the night was over, they came over to us. I was surprised, but I played it cool. I didn't want to seem like the desperate type. We all chatted in a group for a few minutes; the club was about to close down by the time they made it over to us. The tall, handsome man I wanted, introduced himself as Trevor. He went on to introduce his friends as well. After introductions, we talked about only God knows what because I don't remember. All I remember is that I could not take my eyes off him, and I was hoping he would ask for my phone number. Well, instead of asking for my number, he asked if we wanted to go hang out a while longer. I didn't get a bad vibe from him; I wanted to go. I looked at Dionne, begging with my eyes for her to say yes. When she said yes, I jumped up and down on the inside but kept my composure. We ended up going back to Trevor's apartment with him and his friends.

His apartment was a two-bedroom, one-and-a-half

bathroom, townhome located in Starkville. It was surprisingly clean and in order, which was impressive. It didn't smell like the typical bachelor's pad. The walls were white and bare. There was a sofa positioned against the longest wall to the left, along with a small table in the middle of the floor. The television was on a stand positioned against the wall opposite the sofa, so we could sit on the sofa and watch television without straining our necks. The stairs leading up to the bedrooms were directly in front of the door. There was a half bath with a toilet, sink, and mirror downstairs, located just before entering the kitchen. The bathroom was also clean, with no rings in the toilet. I was pleased to see how clean the bathroom was. It wasn't spotless, but it wasn't disgusting, either.

    Trevor was also quite the gentleman. He and his friends were all gentlemen. They offered us something to drink and eat. Dionne and I had water. I sat next to Dionne on the couch. Trevor was across the room on the floor. We were all talking and having a good time. There wasn't anything inappropriate being said or done. I was feeling this guy. I wanted to get to know him better. When we got on the subject of church and the Bible, I knew there was more to him than met the eye. He knew a lot. It was obvious he grew up in the church. After we all had been talking for what seemed like hours, Trevor walked into the kitchen with his friend, Shun.

    When they came back into the living room, Trevor sat on the floor next to my knees. I was still sitting on the couch with my sister. I knew he was interested in me, but I didn't want to get my hopes up because he still hadn't officially asked me for my number. I pretended not to notice the closeness of his body to mine, but inside, I was beaming. We all kept talking and laughing, and before long, he was asking me if I had a boyfriend. *Yippee!* He finally asked! I was more than happy to tell him that I was single with no prospects. I wanted to know him and go as far as we could go together. By the end of the night, I found out he was about seven years older than me. I couldn't believe it. He had such a babyface. I thought for sure he was eighteen or nineteen years old. Before we left his apartment, he asked for my phone number. I was more than happy to give it to him.

I hated playing the waiting game, but after a day he called me. The conversations we had weren't boring; I foresaw that we would be good together. After a few days, I told him I had a daughter. I told him about her birth father and the culmination of our relationship. I was expecting him to say, "Okay, it was nice knowing you," but he didn't. He didn't seem to be bothered by it. He said he hoped to meet her one day.

I was still at a stance in my life, where I felt I wasn't good enough because I had a child because that was what I had been told, and a part of me still believed it. I was still carrying around a lot of hurt, but I hid it well. Mom raised me to never show signs of weakness, so I buried my feelings about a lot of things all of the time.

***

As I said before, I started attending a new church in the fall of my freshman year. The name of that church is Peter's Rock Temple Church of God in Christ. My Uncle Charlie and his family had been long-time members. I wanted to try a new way of doing church from the way I had grown up. I had been hurt during my pregnancy at the church I grew up in, and I wanted to get away from it. Other than my mom and sister still being members, I had no ties there. My pain kept me from seeing the good in the people there. It

Resilient

wasn't that I hated them; it was just that I didn't know how to deal with them anymore. To be respectful, I spoke when I was spoken to. But deep down inside, I wanted to tell some of them to get out of my face. Nobody should have to experience that kind of judgment. They were not God! Yet, I saw, felt, and heard the judgment every time I walked through those doors on Sunday while I was pregnant. Isn't church the go-to place for the broken?

Anyway, I started attending my uncle's church; I must say I loved it. The church was beautifully decorated. The sanctuary was big enough for about 300 people or more. There was red carpet throughout the sanctuary. The wooden pews with red fabric were separated by a center aisle with some on the left and others on the right. There was a balcony upstairs for overflow seating. Sometimes the overflow area wasn't enough because the church was full just about every Sunday with college students from Mississippi State University (MSU), others from the community, and families, who had been members for years.

Church service was always spirit-filled. I loved the sound of the drums, guitar, organ, and handclapping. The dancing and shouting were refreshing to me. There was never an usher around trying to calm someone down when they felt like praising God. We were free to worship and praise as we pleased, and that was music to my ears. After a while, I joined the church. I took all of my hurt and pain with me. I told Trevor I had joined. He thought it was great, but he grew up Baptist like I did, and Baptist was where he was going to stay. We went to church together a few times, but I think he enjoyed the atmosphere of the Baptist church more.

Trevor knew a lot about the Bible. He'd read it, I'm sure, in its entirety. I asked him once if he had been called to preach. He laughed and said, "Absolutely not!"

I beg to differ. I believe preaching and teaching is something he had been running from. To this day, I'm waiting for him to do his first sermon. Even today, when I think of him, I smile. Although our relationship didn't work out the way I had wanted, we were still good. He was still loving, and so was I. We had great times. When I look back, the good in him outweighed the bad.

12

Trevor loved Ariel and treated her as his own. He loved her, and she loved him. His family loved her and me! They were always welcoming and kind. I clearly remember when Trevor's mom, Kathleen met Ariel and me. She didn't flinch. I didn't see a moment of judgment written on her face.

She picked Ariel up, hugged her, and walked away with her like she had known Ariel for her whole life. I fell in love with Mrs. Jones that day. Trevor's sisters were kind and loving toward Ariel and me, as well. So was his dad. I loved the love that was there.

After we had been dating a while, things started to go left. Trevor said, "You're too young for me, and we want different things. I have to get my shit together." It came out of nowhere. It hurt me to hear it, but I knew he was telling the truth. I figured he was in a slump then, but things would turn around. He loved me. I knew he did; he just felt like he wasn't good for me.

After he told me this, I took it at face value and decided to be okay with it. I saw where he stood. I wasn't going to try to make him stay with me. By the time this occurred, I moved out of the apartment I shared with my mom and got my own place. It just happened to be in the same apartment complex he had moved to. I could see his apartment, and he could see mine. It was my first apartment, and it wasn't in the best shape. But it was mine, and I could afford it. Mom didn't want me to move in over there, but it was time to get my apartment like I'd intended to do in the first place. It was two bedrooms with one bathroom located on the second floor. I wasn't too keen on having someone live above me, so I wanted to be on the second floor. There was a problem with roaches there, but it wasn't too bad. I found one dead or saw one crawling just about every day, though ... Ugh! One day, things would have to get better.

Anyway, like I was saying before, I took what he said at face value and understood he didn't want to be in a committed relationship. So, I decided to let things be and move on. Well, a while back, I'd met this guy named, Jonathan, at a Club 124 in Starkville. Club 124 was where the college students hung out. There was always a party there on Friday or Saturday nights. I'd gone out with Dionne to have a good time. I told Jonathan I was in a relationship, and I did not need any new friends. He understood, and that was that. We happened to cross paths again at the same club, but this time, I gave him my phone number. We started talking on the phone, but we hadn't gone out on a date.

One night, he asked me out. But I had an exam coming up. I told him to come over to my place and hang out, so I could study, too. I put Ariel to bed before he got there because I didn't want her randomly meeting people. I had him come over later—after she fell into a deep sleep.

Maybe thirty minutes after he got there, we heard banging on the door. It scared the crap out of me. I looked through the peephole. It was Trevor! *What the heck?*

I went to close Ariel's bedroom door, hoping she wouldn't hear the noise. I called through the door, "What do you want?"

He yelled, "Open the door!"

Oh, no! I was not about to open that door unless my life depended on it. I yelled back, "Go home!"

"I ain't going no damn where! Open the door!"

"Go home!"

By this time, Jonathan was getting upset. He said to open the door. I said, "No, absolutely not. Let his ass stay out there; he'll eventually go home."

Trevor kept banging, but I didn't budge. I heard Trevor's friends outside the door. What in the world was really going on here? More banging on the door.

"Open the door, Robin!"

"No, I'm not opening the door!"

"You got another nigga in there; you better open this damn door!" Then Trevor kicked the door.

"You basically told me you didn't want to be with me, so why are you here?"

Jonathan picked up his phone. He was about to call his fraternity brothers to come over to fight Trevor and his friends. *Wait! What? Not today! Not today! My daughter is here!* I told Jonathan, "Put your phone down."

Then there was silence. I assumed Trevor had walked away.

By this time, Ariel was wide awake. She wasn't crying, but she sure was trying to figure out what was going on. Her three-year-old brain was confused, especially at seeing a guy she'd never seen before, which pissed me off! *Shit!*

"Robin, open the door! This is Patricia!" I heard Trevor's cousin.

"No, Patricia! I don't know what he's going to do, and Ariel is here."

"He's not going to do anything. I sent him back to the apartment. He just wants to talk to you. That's it."

I looked through the peephole and saw Patricia. I looked out the window and saw Trevor had left. I opened the door. She came inside. I was holding Ariel so that she wouldn't be afraid. I told Patricia, "I'm going to tell Jonathan to leave, but I don't want any trouble in the parking lot."

I guess Jonathan sent a text to some of his boys. By the time he got out there, they were already outside. Wherever they were, it wouldn't have taken them long to get to my place. Starkville is not that big, and there are apartments all over the place for college students.

"Are you sure you're going to be all right?" Jonathan asked.

I looked at Patricia, then back at him, and said, "Yeah, I'll call you later." With that, he left.

After he left, Patricia left. Then I closed and locked my door. I sat down on my couch and held Ariel until she was just about asleep again. Then there was a knock at the door. I got up, carrying Ariel along with me, and asked who was at the door. And, of course, it was Trevor.

I opened the door and stood in the doorway, blocking his

entrance. He looked and smelled like he had been drinking too much alcohol, which wasn't unusual for him. I didn't say anything. I stared at him. He asked if he could come in, and I moved aside. Ariel laid her head down on my shoulder and was sound asleep. I'm glad she was tired that night. Trevor walked in and stood in the middle of the living room, waiting for me to close the door.

 I turned to look at him, waiting for him to say something since I didn't have anything to say. I was irritated, and I didn't want to be bothered with him. I was tired of his excessive drinking. I was tired of his friends being around all the time. I was tired of him not being everything I needed him to be for Ariel and me. I loved him, but I saw where our relationship was going. It was going nowhere. He'd basically told me I was too young for a serious relationship; so there wasn't a need for me to invest anymore time and energy. I just didn't know how to say it.

 He still didn't say anything; he took Ariel from my arms and held her close to him, hugging her, and rocking from side to side. She didn't budge. I saw the love he had for her. Then he carried her to her room, put her in her bed, and came back out. He hugged me and apologized. He slept at my apartment that night. He held me until we fell asleep.

***

 After about three months, I broke my lease and moved out of that apartment and moved back in with my mom until I could find a cleaner place. The landlord understood. He knew that complex needed a lot of work. He didn't charge me any extra for getting out of my lease early. I didn't plan to live with my mom long. I put all of my furniture in storage. I slept on the floor or the couch in her living room, and Ariel slept in the bed with Mom.

One Saturday night, I had gone out clubbing with Dionne. We had a great time, as usual, and my mom kept Ariel, as usual. Mom didn't like us going out like that, but since Dionne and I were always together to look out for each other, she didn't make too much of a fuss. We stayed out late that night like we normally did. When I got home, I made a pallet on the floor. I was too tired to shower. I just wanted to go to sleep. Early the next morning, I heard someone say, "Robin!" I slowly opened my eyes to peek through my eyelashes, but I didn't move. "Robin! I got something I want you to do!"

I immediately sat up and looked to my left and then to my right. The apartment was quiet. I yelled out, "Mama, did you call me?"

"No," she said, still half asleep.

"Are you sure?" I asked, jumping off the floor to go to her room. "You just said you had something you want me to do."

"I did not."

"I heard you loud and clear, Mom."

"That was not me. It was God talking to you because I've been sleep."

I walked out of her room with my head held down thinking, *Whatever, not me. I'm only nineteen years old.* I brushed it off and went back into the living area to lay down on the floor. I couldn't get what just happened out of my mind, though. *Was that really God calling me? Why me? I'm no good.*

***

Trevor and I were together for about two years. I loved him. I wanted to be with him. I thought we would eventually end up getting married. But the longer we were together, the further apart we became. We were on two different wavelengths. He wanted to drink and hang out with his friends every weekend, and I was looking forward to graduating from college to go to pharmacy school. He dropped out of school, but he remained in the National Guard. He quit for financial reasons. I suppose staying in the military was good for him. I wished he would have just gotten a student loan to pay for the tuition cost remaining after the National Guard paid their part.

He said more than once, "I'm not ready for you." Trevor also once told me, "I'm not in a good place. I can't provide for you. I feel like less than a man because of my financial problems. I'm trying to get it figured out. I had to sell my granddad's horses. Do you know how hard that was for me?" I watched him drown his pain and disappointment in alcohol. I couldn't stand it. He was a good man. He'd have a bright future if he changed his way of thinking. I wanted so badly to help him, but I couldn't.

I was in no better position than he was. I used my refund checks from school to pay my rent up through the end of each semester. I received food stamps to get grocery, and that wasn't enough because it was less than $100 a month. I had a harder time getting government assistance than women sitting at home every day. I applied for a housing voucher, but I was put on waiting list; I never heard back from them. I applied for Temporary Assistance for Needy Families (TANF), but I was denied because I couldn't volunteer during the day. I told my social worker I was in college, going to school full time during the day and couldn't volunteer. She said, "It's a requirement," then denied me. I was denied Medicaid, but Ariel could get it, so I was satisfied with that. Ariel was also on my mom's insurance; I made my mother her legal guardian just in case something happened to me (for a moment I had considered going to the Air Force). Thank God, I was able to remain on my mom's health insurance because I was a college student. I worked my work-study job and a part-time job as a pharmacy technician at Wal-Mart and then Walgreens to have extra money to pay for lights, gas, clothing, food that food stamps didn't cover, etc. My parents provided me with a car, so I didn't have to worry about transportation. To save money, I started washing and styling my hair myself. I didn't go to the nail salon to get pedicures or my nails done. I started taking care of those needs myself. I could not afford to do a lot of things I saw a lot of young ladies my age doing. I was focused on taking care of my daughter; making sure we had a roof over our heads. Even though times were hard, I thanked God because things could have been worse. I cried sometimes. Words cannot express how frustrated I was, but I refused to give up.

As much as I wanted to help Trevor, and as much as he wanted to help me, we couldn't help each other. We each had our own set of issues. We held on as long as we could. He felt like I was too young to be in a serious relationship. I felt like he drank too much. He loved Ariel, but he wasn't ready to take on the responsibility of taking care of us. Over time, we started talking less and less. We also saw less of each other. I was in a place where I was trying to make better choices and set goals for myself. Although we loved each other, love wasn't enough to keep us together.

Around the time that my relationship with Trevor was dwindling, I met this guy, named Brandon, at MUW. He worked for the Mississippi School for Math and Science on MUW's campus. I had just pledged Delta Sigma Theta Sorority, Inc. in the spring of 2002. I met him early 2003 through my line sister, Tasha. Brandon was about twenty-six years old, had already graduated from college with his bachelor's degree. He was also a minister, and in his own way, he was kind of cute. I talked to him from time to time, and I enjoyed his company. I started talking to him more often while talking to Trevor less often. Trevor was with his friends all of the time. I didn't like to be around them so much, especially with Ariel being small. If he wasn't alone, then more than likely, I wasn't going to see him that day.

Juggling motherhood as a single mom and going to college was enough in itself, but I wanted to get married and have a family. I didn't want to wear the "single mom" label or the "baby mama" label, or even the "teen mom" label. Those were labels I was ashamed of. I felt shame for a long time, longer than I should have. I was on a mission to change that. As a result, I remained in a relationship that was no longer working, hoping it would turn into something more. *Crazy right?* I wasn't emotionally, spiritually, or financially ready for marriage. I was in love with the idea of love. I was in love with the idea of marriage. I wanted the fairytale.

The turning point came for Trevor and me after his biological father died. He was very upset about his father's death, although he tried to hide it. I think Trevor had unfinished business with him. There were a lot of things he wanted to say as well as a lot of questions he wanted answered. However, I'm not sure that he got a chance to have that conversation. Their relationship had been strained over the years.

While our relationship was practically over, I still went to the funeral with him for moral and emotional support. In the middle of the pastor's eulogy, he did something unorthodox for a funeral service. Trevor got up and walked out. He walked across the front of the church, past the casket, and out the side door. I sat there dumbfounded, trying to figure out if I should go after him or stay. I went with the former. After about a minute of debate, I went after him through the same door.

I found him in the fellowship hall, sitting at a table with his back turned to the entrance. I knew he was upset, but I didn't have the words to comfort him. I stood there for a moment and decided to walk over to him. I didn't say a word at first. I just sat down beside him, put my hand on his back, and asked, "Are you all right?"

He brushed it off and said, "Yeah, it's all good. I'm all right."

I didn't believe him, of course, but I sat there until he was ready to go back in. I don't even remember if we went back inside the sanctuary or not. I do remember not leaving his side until the funeral and repass were over. Speaking of repass, he met the woman he would eventually marry that day at the repass. She was a friend of his cousin, Patricia. She sat down at the same table with us, directly across from Trevor. Instantly, I sensed her attraction to him. I looked at him and sensed he was attracted to her as well. The funny thing was I didn't even get upset. I smiled inside knowing that he would soon be happy again. I already knew our relationship was over.

Neither of us could work up the nerve to say the words to end it. After I left the church, I didn't call him, and he didn't call me. One day of no calls turned into two, and two into three, and before we knew it, it had been over a month since we'd spoken. That's not an acceptable way to end a relationship, but when there isn't any reason in particular other than knowing it's over, there isn't anything left to say.

13

Meanwhile, I'd run into Ariel's dad every now and then. One time, in particular, I will never forget. I happened to see him at the mall. He was standing with a couple of guys talking. I could have kept walking like I didn't see him, but I decided to be the mature one and speak. As I walked up to him, I noticed how nicely he was dressed. He had on diamond earrings, or at least they looked like diamonds. He had on a blinged-out watch, nice looking sneakers, and was dressed very well in brand named clothing. He was clean from head to toe. All I could think was, *Wow! If only he made sure his daughter looked this good!* All of my money was going toward caring for her. Where was his part? I was seething inside, ready to explode on him. But the last time I did that, innocent people got hurt in the process, including myself. So, I decided against that.

As I stood directly in front of him, I said, "Hello."

He replied with the same.

One of the guys asked him who I was, and he said, "Oh, she's my baby's mama."

I cringed at the sound of those words coming from his mouth, but I said nothing. He asked, "How is Ariel doing?"

I replied, "Fine."

Then, instead of pulling money out of his pocket to put in my hands, he said, "If you ever need anything, just call me."

That's when I wanted to pop off on Austin and say, *Ariel needs something every damn day! She needs clothes, food, crayons, diapers, a roof over her head, lights, water, and a source of transportation. I'm over here taking care of this baby by my damn self, and you're living like you don't have a care in the world! You don't give a damn about her because if you did, you would at least pay the little ass $25 the court ordered you to pay when she was born, and we don't even get that shit! Fuck you!*

But instead, I held all of that in and walked away mad and frustrated. I wasn't about to call him for anything. Why would I call him when he'd never come through for me when she needed anything before? There was an incident when Ariel had gotten a sore in her head that wouldn't heal. I took her to a dermatologist. Before he would see her, I had to pay ninety-seven dollars because the office did not accept Medicaid. I called Austin to tell him I needed money for the doctor's visit. I figured since he was not helping me with anything else, the least he could do was help me pay for her to see the doctor. He told me he did not have any money. He had money for anything he wanted, though.

To top all of that off, the ninety-seven dollars I paid that day to the dermatologist was a waste of money because the antibiotic did not work. After a few days of treatment, the sore was getting worse and she started losing hair. So, I took her to her pediatrician's office.

She saw Dr. Cain that day. He basically accused me of being an unfit mother because Ariel's hair was falling out. He asked, "Why did you wait so long to bring her to the doctor?" I told Dr. Cain, I had already taken to her a dermatologist who had given her an antibiotic. His irritation shifted away from me toward the dermatologist. Dr. Cain said Ariel was misdiagnosed. She had a fungus in her head. He prescribed an antifungal medication for her take orally every day for six weeks.

As I walked backed through the mall toward my car, I made up my mind to no longer worry about what he was or wasn't doing to help me. I had to change my focus to what I had to do to help me. I had to make sure Ariel and I would not always struggle, and I wanted to do it the right way. I had never been the type to run behind a man for his money. I wasn't attracted to the dope boy life. It wasn't that I couldn't have them; men approached me all the time ready and willing to give me money. But what would it cost me? It would cost me my integrity. It would cost me my peace. It would cost me many sleepless nights. If I was going to lose sleep, it was going to be because I was up studying or working to take care of my business.

***

Austin got married before I graduated from MUW. I found out he was seriously dating someone when I had gone to the April's dormitory to pick Ariel up. This girl named Charmaine got on the elevator with Ariel and me (and some other girls) when we were headed back down to the car. I had no idea who she was. She didn't say anything to me, but she was talking to Monica, someone I knew from campus. Charmaine kept giving me the side-eye. *What the fuck is her problem?* When Charmaine got off the elevator, Monica said, "Do you know who she is?"

"No."

"She told me Ariel is going to be her step-daughter."

"What?"

"Yeah, she go with Ariel daddy."

"Well if she thinks she's got something, more power to her. I don't want his ass."

Monica laughed, and Ariel and I proceeded to my vehicle to leave campus. Months later before Austin got married, he came by my apartment to see me. He told me he wanted to talk to me about something.

"I'm getting married."

"Congratulations," I said, but didn't mean it.

"I still love you Robin. If you tell me today that you want to be with me, I'll call this wedding off today. I'll do it right now." Then, he pulled me close and kissed me. I didn't have the same feelings as he did. I was still holding on to hurt he inflicted upon me in the past. Not to mention, he was a shitty father. That didn't help his case.

"I'll always love you Austin, but we can't be together." If Austin had just shown some interest in being a father and being present in Ariel's life, I would have been willing to give him what he wanted. Austin left and not too long after that conversation, he got married. From what I was told, he had a beautiful wedding. I dropped Ariel off at the wedding. I didn't get her hair styled or buy her new clothes for the wedding. I felt if he wanted her to be beautiful for his big day, he needed to make sure she was dressed for the occasion.

Austin got to go off and be happy, while I was still left to struggle on my own. I asked God, *Why does he get to be happy and be made out to be father of the year, while I do everything by myself? That's not fair. It's not fair to me or Ariel. I know he was young when I got pregnant, but so was I. Why do I have to bear the burden alone?* For a while after he was married, he asked for Ariel to come over more. I didn't object. I wanted her to have a relationship with her dad. I didn't want to get in the way of that. In the beginning, I would pack up clothes for her and stuff to do her hair. Then, I had an epiphany. I said, "Robin, girl if he wants to be father of the year, let him! Stop packing up bags of clothes, panties, and shoes that you bought to send over there. Let him buy her what she needs to keep at his place. You doin' too much! Let's see what he is gonna do!"

So, I stopped sending her things over there. If he wanted her to come, then he needed to buy her some clothes. He was barely paying child support. I'd gone to court for about our child support case in 2002 or 2003. While I was granted an increase, I rarely received the checks. He wasn't doing anything else to care for her. So, that was his chance to do what he needed to do as a father. Turns out, he didn't buy her any clothes or shoes when she went over there. She came back home in the same clothes that I would send her in. I asked her, "Ari did your daddy get you any clean clothes to put on?"

"No ma'am."

"Oh okay."

"Mama, Charmaine is mean to me. I don't want to go back to daddy's house."

"Mean like what baby?"

"She's always yelling at me and just make me sit down and not do anything."

"Where is your daddy when you're over there?"

"He is always gone."

"Ok, well sweetheart, I won't make you go back if you don't want to."

"Thank you," Ariel said with a smile.

"Give mommy a hug."

She hugged me. I held on to her tightly and kissed her cheek. *That sorry ass excuse of a man!* I was prepared to tell Austin what Ariel said the next time he called and asked for her to come over, but he didn't call. I didn't call him either. What was the point?

14

After my relationship with Trevor ended, I was in another relationship in no time. I started dating Brandon. Although he wasn't my usual type, I liked him. I felt like he would be good for me. He wasn't a constant drinker like Trevor was. He had money saved. He drove a 2003 Lincoln LS. He appeared to have his life together. To top all of that off, he was a minister. I thought he could help me spiritually, and I would grow closer to God in the process. Well, I did grow closer to God, but it wasn't because he helped me; it was because he almost destroyed me.

Being in a relationship with him was one of the darkest times of my life. Let me tell you why …

Being that I was young and restless, I didn't take the time I needed to heal from my relationship with Trevor. I didn't take the time I needed to reflect and sort out my feelings about my life. Everyone needs that time, even though we don't always take it. I remember always feeling like I wasn't good enough like I wasn't worthy. I had baggage from my past going into the relationship with Brandon that I still hadn't dealt with. He only added to it.

I remember, one night, I was at Brandon's place; it's a night I'll never forget. Brandon lived on campus in the dorms because he worked with the Mississippi School for Mathematics and Science. His job provided housing for him right on campus. Like most dormitories, he shared a bathroom with an adjacent room. That night, I was going to stay over with him. I went into the bathroom to take a shower. I left the bathroom door cracked just in case someone came into the bathroom from the other side, he could hear me if something happened. I thought I was erring on the side of caution by leaving the door cracked, but it turned out I left the door open for him to hurt me instead of protect me.

While I was in the shower, he came into the bathroom naked and got into the shower with me.

I asked, "What are you doing?"

He didn't say anything. He pushed me against the shower wall and lifted my leg.

"No, stop it!"

He still didn't say a word. His penis was hard; he was ready. The water was hot and steamy, which I assumed turned him on even more because he just shoved himself inside me, started pumping, and grinding until he was satisfied. I kept telling him to stop. It was painful, and my body wasn't responding. I don't see how he got pleasure from it.

When he was finished, he took a quick shower and got out. I remember he was talking while he was cleaning himself off, but I can't recall any of what he said. I was still standing there in shock.

I couldn't believe what had just happened to me. I didn't know how to feel. I was at a loss for words. All I could think was, *Did he just rape me? Did this really happen to me?*

After he got out, I remained in the shower for I don't know how long. I had mixed emotions and many thoughts going through my mind. *Did I do something to make him think I wanted this? Was I supposed to yell, kick, and scream for him to hear me? Was it rape since I knew him? He didn't have my consent, though ... I told him no more than once? What should I do now? I need to get the hell out of here!*

I can't remember anything else from that night. I don't know if I stayed or if I left. The only thing I remember is calling April, my best friend, and telling her what had happened. She asked, "Why didn't you scream or yell?"

I didn't have an answer. No should mean no, especially when it's a man who is not a stranger to me. She said, "You need to talk to him about what happened just to see where his mind is and tell him what you're feeling to make sure it doesn't happen again."

While I was talking to her, I heard the sirens going off in my head telling me to RUN, RUN, RUN! I never wanted to speak to him again. But against my better judgment, I did talk to him. Long story short, he said he thought I wanted to have sex because I didn't lock the bathroom door. I told him I said no repeatedly.

He said, "I thought you were just playing hard to get." That was such crap, but I thought maybe it was my fault for even being there in the first place, for taking a shower. So, I did what most women do. I blamed myself. I took the blame and continued to see him.

As time went on, I got to know his family and a couple of

his friends. The first time I met his mother, I went alone. I didn't take Ariel with me because even then, there was still a stigma associated with teenage mothers. I can't say how many times I received a judging look from people who didn't even know me. So, I left Ariel behind with my mother, I guess. I don't quite remember who she was with. We pulled up to a nice, well maintained, double-wide mobile home. I was puzzled because I didn't expect his parents to live in a mobile home. He explained that his mom had turned their house into a childcare center, and they were living in the mobile home until they could get a new house built.

When I walked into the kitchen, where she was, she looked me up and down from head to toe and frowned, but she quickly tried to hide it by replacing it with a smile. I suspected she wasn't pleased. I was slightly offended because there was nothing wrong with what I had on. My hair was neatly done, I had on very little make-up (I like a natural look), a nice pair of jeans, and a blouse that revealed nothing. I was appropriately dressed.

"How are you doing? Come on in," she said with a smile that didn't meet her eyes. I walked into the kitchen and sat down at the table. Brandon was fast behind me. Instead of sitting, he stood, leaning against the wall. I sensed she thought her son was too good for me. It was written all over her face. Little did she know, her son had already forced himself on me and berated me before she ever laid eyes on me.

"It's nice to meet you." I wanted to reach out for a handshake or hug or something, but she had her hands clasped together in her lap. This indicated something I had been taught early on; when people do that during a greeting, they don't want to shake hands or give a hug. So, I kept my hands and arms to myself.

"It's nice to meet you, too. Where are you from?"

"West Point."

"What do your parents do?"

"My dad is a pharmacist, and my mom is a nurse."

"Do you go to church?"

"Yes, ma'am."

"Where you go to church at?"

"Peter's Rock Church of God in Christ."

"Oh, ok."

"She has a daughter, too," Brandon chimed in.

"You have a daughter?" she asked in utter shock. She displayed a look of contempt that she could not hide. It's hard to explain, but I suddenly felt shame. Maybe, just maybe, I wasn't good enough for her son. After all, I had baggage. Obviously, she didn't want her son helping me carry it.

"Yes, ma'am."

"How old is she?"

"Four."

"What's her name?"

"Ariel," I said, looking down into my lap. I could no longer take the scrutiny looking at her face to face. I felt so small. I don't think she was trying to make me feel that way, but I felt as if I didn't belong. In her defense, I'd felt that way since I went to the doctor and saw Ariel's little heartbeat on the monitor. I had felt out of place and lost since that day.

"That's a pretty name," she said. "I'd like to meet her one day."

I peeked up at her in disbelief. I had not expected her to say that. After all of the questions, I was ready to get out of there. So, I said, "Yes, ma'am." I was relieved and exhaled the breath I had been holding. She changed the subject and started talking to her son.

Brandon had two sisters, Andrea and Maggie. They were great. Both of them were nurses, already excelling in their careers. Although we were different in a few ways, basically in the way we dressed, we were alike in many other ways. Neither of them pretended to be perfect like Brandon did. Neither of them led the life their parents wanted for them. Neither of them made me feel small. They were always cordial to me. For the daughters to be so genuine, I didn't see how his parents could raise a selfish and hypocritical son. I have many memories about how unkind and cruel he was to me.

For example, we were out late one night, and he brought up Ariel. He said that he wanted me to leave Ariel with her dad and let Austin raise her. *Wait. What? Does he really think I would choose him over my child? He must be crazy!*

"Why won't you let her daddy raise her?"

"Because she is my daughter, and I'm her mother. I'm going to raise her!"

"I don't really want a kid around," Brandon said in a pragmatic tone.

"I don't care! Ari is my baby, and we are a package deal! If you don't want her around, you don't want me around."

I was beyond upset! After I said that, he didn't say anything. I think he was in disbelief I'd spoken to him that way. I didn't care. I didn't play then, and I don't play now when it comes to my children.

To Brandon's family, he was a God-ordained minister, a true man of God. He lived right. He loved the Lord, and he was a caring man who treated people kindly. That's not the person I saw when I looked at him. That's not the person I knew. He had shown me time and time again who he was. He stomped on my dreams of becoming a pharmacist; he told me lies about my family and friends not loving me; he was verbally and emotionally abusive, and he shattered my self-esteem. He wanted me all to himself. Once, he said I didn't need anybody but him, which is why he often tried alienating me from my family and friends. Quite a few times, he forced himself on me for sex. I can't fathom how he obtained pleasure from it; my body did not respond to his advances. He would have sex with me anyway, and it was painful. I was always sore for a few days afterward. He didn't care. He treated me badly, but I stayed. I wanted out of the relationship, but I didn't know how to get out of it. He exerted control over me.

    I must admit it was because of this relationship that I drew closer and closer to God. I needed God to help me. I needed Jesus to save me from myself. I needed the Holy Spirit to guide me. I was a lost soul, trying to find my way. My circumstances were making it harder to see God working in my life. I wanted to see the promises I had read about in Scripture, but everything was foggy.

***

    I graduated from college at twenty-one years old, in August 2003. I was proud of myself. I'd set out to do something, and I had done it. I graduated with a 3.4-grade point average (GPA), or maybe it was 3.3, I don't remember. I was glad to see it. I didn't study all of the time like I should have. I held down two jobs while going to school, paid rent and utilities, woke up early, and stayed up late many days to get to where I was. I was thankful, appreciative, and grateful to God I had succeeded. April and I graduated at the same time. We cried a flood of tears that day because she was leaving to go back home to Chicago. She was my best friend, and I was going to miss her. I would miss talking all of the time and ditching class to hang out at the Lock & Dam in Columbus. I would miss having her around to study and laugh with. Over my last two years at the W, she had become a major part of my life. I didn't know what I'd do without her.

Before graduation, I'd applied to pharmacy school at the University of Mississippi, also known as Ole Miss, and had been rejected. I was disappointed. I didn't know what I was going to do next, but I had to do something. I had to remain in college to stay on my mom's healthcare insurance; I had to go back to school. I enrolled at Mississippi State University. I didn't major in anything. I just took random undergraduate courses I had interest in. Hindsight is 20/20. What I should have done was enroll in graduate school in Master of Business Administration program, but I wasn't thinking like that back then. I needed to be in college taking anything, so that's what I did.

Amid all of the changes and disappointment of rejection from Ole Miss I was experiencing, I found out I was pregnant. When I found out, I was about eight or nine weeks along. I had been taking birth control but not consistently. Hence, the pregnancy. *How could I let this happen?* All I thought was I did not want to marry Brandon; I also didn't want to be a single mother with two "baby daddies." I told my mom about the pregnancy. I was upset. Brandon wasn't all that he portrayed himself to be. I was in a relationship that wasn't good for me, and I did not want to deal with him for the rest of my life. I told my mom I didn't want to marry him. She reassured me that I did not have to marry him just because I was pregnant. *Who is going to want to be with me with two children?* There was no light, only darkness.

Soon after I found out about my pregnancy, Brandon and I went out to lunch. I had to work up the nerve to tell him. When I told him about my pregnancy, his tune changed. We ended up having a heated conversation. I wasn't thrilled about the pregnancy either, but I wanted to keep the baby. I couldn't see myself getting an abortion. That was a road I didn't want to travel. When I told him I was pregnant, he said, "I don't want you to have that bastard."

"I'm having it! I'm going to tell your mom about the baby, and I'm going to have it." I said matter-of-factly.

"You tell my mom about that baby, and I'm going to run you over with my car. So, there will be no you and no baby," he said sardonically.

What the hell? Did this man just threaten to kill the baby and me because he doesn't want his mother to know? Is he more concerned about his image than me?

I was speechless. I knew I could not have his baby. There was no way in hell I would deal with such an evil man for the rest of my life. If I had this baby, he would forever be a thorn in my side. I would never be rid of him.

***

Meanwhile, my best friend was now living back in Chicago. But while we were still in college at MUW, I made an effort to buy books and read material that spoke life back into me. One of the first books I read was *Sassy, Single, & Satisfied* by Michelle McKinney Hammond. I also ready *No More Sheets* by Juanita Bynum, and *A Woman After God's Own Heart* by Elizabeth George, to name a few.

God directed me to those books as I walked up and down the aisles of Books-A-Million. April and I read these books together and talked about them. We went through devotions and Bible study materials together. It's like God knew I would need April when I met her. I had prayed for so long for a friend I could be myself with. A friend I could talk to about any and everything. God answered my prayers when he brought April into my life in January 2001. April told me about Juanita Bynum's *No More Sheets* sermon on video. I found the VHS and watched it one night after I put Ariel to bed.

Let me tell you, that sermon blew my mind! I have no other words; it blew my mind! I had never seen or heard anybody break down sex and relationships like that. Juanita Bynum opened my eyes to the spiritual stronghold sex and relationships can have on a person. It was a phenomenal lesson. It changed my life and my view on relationships. After I saw this video, I bought her book.

It was hard not having April there with me. We talked on the phone every day, but I needed her more than ever when I found out about my pregnancy. I wanted her to be present with me because I felt alone. In her absence, my line sister, Tracy was there for me. I found no judgement in April's voice or in Tracy's eyes. What more could I ask for?

Resilient through the Pain....

15

The following Monday, I called an abortion clinic in Alabama. As much as I hated it, I had made the decision not to have the baby. It hurt me, but it seemed like the best thing to do. I was still young and pregnant by a prick! I would be an unwed mother of two, and that wasn't what I wanted for myself. To top it off, Brandon had threatened to kill me if I kept the baby. I wasn't sure he would follow through, but I already had a daughter to live for. I had hopes and dreams I still wanted to live out. When I made the appointment, the nurse said I had to have the abortion before twelve or thirteen weeks. I really can't remember how far along I was, but I do remember there was no time to waste. My mom asked me to let her raise the baby, but I knew that wouldn't work.

On September 13, 2003, Tracy, and I made the drive to Tuscaloosa, Alabama, to abort my unborn child. It was a beautiful morning, warm and breezy. A day like that, I would have normally been glowing and bursting with energy, but that particular Saturday morning, I was feeling down and out. I was disappointed in what I was about to do, but I felt I had no choice. I drove the black Mercury Mountaineer my parents had given me. As we drove, I listened to Maxwell's *This Woman's Work*. I put the CD player on repeat. I played the song over and over because it resonated with my spirit. I let my mind drift back and forth between my past, present, and future. I don't remember talking much on the drive there, but I remember Tracy being supportive. April was gone, and Tracy was all I had left. I couldn't even ask my sister to go with me. She didn't approve. I would have never asked my mom to go, but my sister, I would have expected to be there for me. I felt alone, and Tracy being there made it better. I loved her for that; she was there when I had no one.

When we arrived at the office, I signed in and completed the paperwork; then I paid cash. I was working and still had money left over from my refund check; I was able to pay for the abortion myself. I looked around the waiting room and saw young women, some much younger than me, waiting to get their names called. As I sat there, I wondered if they were feeling the dread I was feeling. It seemed like it took an eternity for them to call me back. When they did, I thought I was going to pass out. My heart was about to jump out of my chest. My stomach was queasy, and I was trembling. Tracy stood up with me; we walked out of the waiting room through the door that led to exam rooms.

I was directed to an exam room by an older, petite nurse. The room was bright and cold. The walls were painted a light grey color. There was a window covered with white blinds, giving the room a little light. The pink examination table was covered with white paper

Resilient

with a disposable pillow underneath. Next to it was a metal lamp with an adjustable head about two or three feet tall.

The nurse gave me a blue paper cover-up and left the room. I removed my bottoms and sat on the table to wait. Tracy remained standing next to me. A middle-aged doctor came in later, rolled the stool from the corner, and took a seat. Before he got started, he asked, "Are you sure you want to move forward?"

I started crying and said, "Yes." I was instructed to lie back on the table and put my feet in the stirrups. As I laid back, staring at the ceiling, my heart was breaking. I had been given some medicine to relax me before the procedure, but I could still feel the panic attack about to overtake me. I was about to do something I never thought I would be doing in a million years. I was in agony. The entire procedure hurled me deeper into my world of depravity. I did not want to go through with it, but I felt I had no other choice. I was pregnant by a man making my life a living hell.

The doctor asked, "Do you already have a child?"

I was quietly sobbing; I couldn't even answer his question. Tracy answered for me as she got some Kleenex to wipe away my tears. She looked at me and said, "Robin, are you sure?"

I still couldn't speak; I nodded my head as I silently cried. The nurse was having a conversation with Tracy about Ariel, but I remained silent. Tracy stood next to me, holding my hand, and wiping my tears as I lay there in anguish. The nurse was standing at my feet, next to the doctor assisting him, doing as she was told.

I cringed at the sound of the vacuum. I wanted to jump off the table and tell him I changed my mind, but my hopelessness for my future held me there. Although the doctor had started the vacuum, he did not immediately start the suctioning. I don't know what he was doing or thinking, but the sound was deafening. It was torturous to my ears, drowning out the debate I was having in my head.

Just when I thought he would never begin, he started sucking the life right out of me. I tried to think of a happier time to escape to, but it wouldn't come. I was taking away a life I had not given. I was taking away a life I had no right to take. *Oh, God, please, forgive me.*

The more he suctioned, the more despair I felt. How was I going to look at myself in the mirror after this? How was God going to love me now? I had added shame on top of shame. I was slightly traumatized and having a hard time processing what was going on, what had just occurred.

After the procedure was done, the nurse said to get dressed. I was zoned out; I still don't remember everything she said to me. I was given a prescription for pain medication and an antibiotic; then I was sent on my way. Tracy drove me home, still listening to *This Woman's Work*. I cried as I drifted in and out of sleep.

***

Even in the midst of all of this, I was still learning how to handle Ariel and her questions about Austin. Ariel often asked me about her dad and when she would see him. I couldn't speak for him. I could have said some not so nice things to her about Austin, but I chose not to do that. Whatever conclusion she would come up with about her biological father as she grew older would be her own and not mine. When she asked for and cried for him, I would hug her and say, "Mommy is here for you. As long as I'm breathing, I will always be here for you. I can't speak for your dad, but you've got me." Even when that wasn't even to soothe her, I would say, "You've got your PawPaw. He loves you! He's all the dad that you need." I'm not sure my words ever helped her hurting heart, but I prayed often that God would take that hurt away.

16

When I arrived home, my mom was standing in the kitchen at the apartment with a look of disappointment. She knew what I had done because I told her what I was going to do. I cried again when I saw her. She hugged me for a few seconds and said, "It's over. You need to suck it up." Yep, she told me to suck it up. So, there was not any comfort there; not the comfort I wanted and needed.

Mom informed me that she, Dad, and Dionne went out to lunch that day. Daddy had inquired about my whereabouts. Mama took it upon herself to tell him I had gone to get an abortion. I was already upset about what I'd done, and on top of that, she chose to blab to Daddy of all people about it? Really? As if I wasn't ashamed enough. That wasn't anything I wanted my father to ever know. It wasn't her story to tell. She had no right to tell it.

Later that evening, I saw my mother deep in thought. It

seemed like she was angry with me, but I also saw melancholy and hurt written all over her face. She was extremely quiet. Then she suddenly started to speak, and there was no mistaking her fury. Mama unleashed all of the anger she had toward Brandon. She called him every devil she could think of. She was cursing and started crying. I had not seen her that angry in a long time. Mom decided she wanted to talk to Brandon's mother to let her know about what I'd done, and why I'd done it. I gave her the phone number, and she proceeded to dial. I sat there and listened as she told Brandon's mom everything, from him not wanting the baby to Brandon threatening to run over me with his car. They were on the phone for maybe fifteen or twenty minutes. When the call was over, my mom felt better while I felt worse. It would be years before I would feel better again.

  I wanted out of the relationship I had with Brandon after the abortion. What was the point of us even being together after that? I knew there was nothing he could say to make me love him and want to be with him again. I wanted a new start. I needed a refreshing. I didn't talk to Brandon for a few days after the ordeal. When I did, he apologized for his behavior. He said he behaved that way because he didn't want to ruin his image and what his parents thought of him. I'm not quite sure how his parents saw him after our moms' conversation because my mom revealed it all.

  Against my better judgment, I decided to give him another chance, even though I knew he wasn't the man for me, and I should have no longer been in the relationship. He was persistent, talked a good game, and I hoped he would change. He said God told him I was his wife. *Maybe I should give it time to see if God will tell me that he is my husband.* I wanted to see what the end would be. That's when the rollercoaster of the ups and downs of me really began.

After our relationship started back up, things were good, but only for a moment. I eventually stopped going to Peter's Rock every Sunday and started going to church on Saturday with him and his family. Brandon's mother and father had started their own church. The church was beautiful from the stained glass to the upholstered purple church pews to the beautiful deep-colored purple carpet. The pulpit was simple enough with just a podium there with an elegant appeal. I don't think I had ever seen such a beautiful sanctuary. I often wondered where they got the money from to build such a beautiful space when the membership only consisted of a maximum of twenty people. The church was large enough to house at least 200 to 300 members, but the membership was lacking. Brandon was from a town smaller than West Point. I don't think there were many middle-class, let alone, rich people living in that town. So for them to have a church so beautifully done was surprising to me. Even the smell in the sanctuary was heavenly.

***

It wasn't long before I found out he'd cheated on me with another young lady at the church. I felt like something was off with my body. I couldn't put my finger on it. I wasn't having any symptoms or a discharge, but something didn't feel right. I went to the emergency room instead of my regular doctor because I was too ashamed to go into the doctor's office.

I told the ER nurse I wanted to be checked for sexually transmitted diseases. The physician assistant came in, performed a vaginal exam, and took samples for the testing. Before I left, I was given some medication to take right there in the ER for chlamydia, gonorrhea, and trichomoniasis. The nurse told me to grab a bite to eat because I would be feeling sick shortly. She wasn't lying. About thirty minutes later, I felt like I was going to vomit. I stopped by The Little Dooey (my favorite BBQ restaurant) to eat. After I sat down to eat, I called April to talk to her about it.

Long story short, a few days later, on Saturday morning while I was at church with Brandon, I got a phone call from the hospital. I walked outside to answer the phone. I was interested to see what the call was about. I wanted to know if I tested positive for any disease. A nurse from the hospital was calling to let me know I had been infected with chlamydia. Just as I'd thought, he had given me a sexually transmitted disease.

I was enraged. I started dating a minister, hoping he could help me with my relationship with Christ. The only thing he was causing me was pain. To add to all the agony that he'd brought into my life, now he had given me a disease.

I was ready to end things with Brandon for good. I remained outside, pacing the rock-filled drive, trying to decide what to do. The weather was nice. The sky was sunny and blue with not an inkling of a cloud. I lifted my face to the sun to feel the warmth as the breeze blew through my hair. I inhaled deeply, trying to gather my thoughts while praying and asking God what I should do. I previously asked God during prayer to give me a sign about Brandon, and He gave it to me. I heard Him loud and clear, telling me to end it. I felt it deep down in my soul. When I opened my eyes, I saw Brandon walking toward me. I guess I didn't come back inside fast enough for him.

"Who were you on the phone with?" he asked in an accusatory tone.

"The hospital!" I went from prayer to pissed in about two point five seconds. How dare he come to me in that manner, demanding to know who I was talking to? His expression faded instantly from hostile to worry. "The nurse just told me that I tested positive for chlamydia. Who have you been having sex with other than me?"

"Nobody," he said convincingly, but I saw the lie all over his face.

"Oh, really? Well, I know I haven't been with anybody else. At my last yearly exam, I was completely healthy, and I've only been with you. It was clean before, and now it's not. I was with you and only you before my yearly and after. This disease doesn't just show up out of thin air. So, who have you been fucking?"

"Well, it was just one time."

I wanted to slap the crap out of him. I had no words. I was furious with him, but most of all with myself because I should have broken things off with him a long time ago. I started walking away; he tried to grab me. I jerked my arm away and yelled, "Don't touch me!"

I started walking back toward the church entrance. If Ariel had not been inside, I would have gotten in my car and left his ass standing in the middle of the parking lot.

I walked back into the church and sat down quietly, fuming, and cursing on the inside. He was on my heel, I'm sure not knowing what to do or say because he was silent. I sat down next to Ariel, trying to pretend everything was all right, but I couldn't wait to get out of there.

This man had already put me through enough. He was an egotistical, self-serving man only out for himself. Where was his integrity? Man of God was what his family called him, but I knew better. I saw a side of him that nobody else could see. I saw through the façade of his fake faith and Christianity with his belief that as long as he looked the part and played the part, all was well with him and God. He was such a hypocrite. He found pleasure in making me feel bad about myself. He found pleasure in having control over me. For the life of me, I could not escape his grasp. I felt like I was stuck even though I had not made any vows of marriage or commitment to him. When I think about it now, I realize it was a stronghold, a soul-tie that only God could break.

After this incident, I knew in my heart of hearts that I had to get away from him. I kept telling myself to break it off; I tried to many times. But each time, he apologized and said that God had brought us together. He continuously said that God told him that I was his wife. He said that he would never let me go.

How could I marry a man like him and be at peace with myself? Marrying him would be like signing my death certificate. By that, I mean death to my hopes and dreams. Death to my joy. Death to my peace of mind. Death to Ariel growing up in a home filled with evidence of overflowing love. I would have none of those things if I remained in a relationship that was literally sucking the life out of me.

During the two-year course of my relationship with Brandon, I had to change who I was. I had to change the me that I was comfortable with. To keep him from talking down to me, especially about my appearance, I had to change the way I dressed. I had to look "holy." He no longer wanted me to wear jeans, make-up, or jewelry. I had to conform to what he wanted me to be. My wardrobe dramatically changed from jeans and t-shirts (what I loved

Resilient

to wear everywhere) to long denim skirts with tennis shoes. I exchanged my hoop earrings for small studs, which I still got flack for, so I decided not to wear earrings at all. I exchanged my natural-looking makeup for a plain face with no glow or appeal.

These changes did not occur overnight. He slowly and strategically molded me into who he wanted me to be. I remember an incident where I went to a church function with him. I wore a black knee-length skirt with a pink and black blouse. I had gotten my hair done into micro-braids. I wanted a little color, so I braided my black tresses with auburn hair. I wore only a little bit of make-up with some lip gloss. The heel of my black Jessica Simpson shoes was about three to four inches high. I looked at myself in the mirror before I left home fully confident, loving what I was looking at.

I met him at the event. While he was working on the mic and speakers on the platform, I was talking with his sister Andrea. I was watching him work, and I admired what he was doing. He was methodical and paying close attention to every detail. He could have passed as a sound engineer instead of a school teacher. I told Andrea, "I'll be right back! I want to go speak to Brandon."

As soon as I walked up to him, he dared to say, "You look like a whore."

In a mere second, he crushed my self-esteem. I looked down at myself, trying to figure out what he saw that I didn't. I did not look like a whore. I was dressed appropriately. I didn't have on too little or too much of anything. I looked at him, wanting to speak up for myself, daring myself to say something. But I had no words. I didn't know what to say. His face was filled with disapproval. I held my head down, turned on my heel, and walked away. When I got back to Andrea. She asked me what happened, and I told her. She said, "Don't listen to him. You are beautiful. He is a jerk." Even though she stood there telling me how beautiful I was, all I thought about was how unbeautiful he made me feel.

***

Brandon tried his best to alienate me from my family by telling me they didn't love me, but I knew they were still there for me. He even told me that there was no way my daddy loved me because he turned his back on me when I got pregnant with Ariel. Brandon wanted me to believe those lies; he was the pot calling the kettle black. By the way he was treating me, he didn't love me either. He told me things like that on more than one occasion.

He tried to drive a wedge between me and my mother as well. Manipulation was a huge part of his game. It took me a while to catch on, but when I did, there was no mistaking his intentions. After I started praying for discernment, God started showing me the spirit of manipulation. That's how I was able to figure it out. I started paying attention to the look in his eyes, his facial expressions, and his demeanor; I noticed the shift every time he was trying to persuade me to stay away from my family and friends.

Only God could help me through everything I was dealing with, and as I continued on my journey to wholeness, I started to change. I didn't want to drink much anymore. I didn't want to smoke. I didn't want to go to the club. I didn't want to have sex. I didn't want to do anything that would get me off the high I was on every time I read the Bible or other reading materials I had picked up from the bookstore. As I walked this walk, I was still in a relationship with Brandon. I was trying to live right and make better choices, yet he made it difficult. One would think that a minister would be supportive of my efforts to be on the right path, but he was only supportive if I was doing what he wanted me to do. He was enthused that I didn't want to go to the club, drink, or smoke anymore, but he wasn't pleased when I didn't want to have sex. So, when I wasn't willing, he forced it.

17

About a year and a half into my relationship with Brandon, we were called into a meeting with the overseer of his family's church. It was a meeting I was not looking forward to. He wanted to speak with us after a church service he had come to town for.

We walked into the office of the church and sat down in the chairs in front of the desk he was sitting behind.

"I want to talk to you two about your relationship. I know you have been dating for a while, and I feel like it's time for you to get married." Pastor Jim said matter-of-factly. "Brandon, I believe that Robin is your wife. God has ordained for the two of you to be together. I just wanted to talk to you about it. Brandon, how do you feel about it?"

"Yes, sir, I have prayed about it. I feel like God is telling me that she is my wife. I already asked her to marry me."

Pastor Jim looked pleased, nodding his head in agreement. Then he looked to me, and said, "Robin, how do you feel about it?"

I didn't know what to say. I had two options. I could tell the truth about how I felt and how I was being treated, or I could lie and say exactly what the pastor wanted to hear. *Tell the truth.* So, I opted for the former and told Pastor Jim the truth.

"Brandon doesn't treat me the way a husband should treat his wife, Pastor Jim." I blurted out before I could stop myself.

"Yes, I do!" Brandon said defensively, frowning in horror and disbelief. He looked like he wanted to melt into the floor. The look on his face was priceless.

"What do you mean by that, Robin?" Pastor Jim interjected before Brandon could say another word.

"He doesn't treat me the way a husband should treat his wife. He is mean to me. He talks down to me. He treats me like an animal. He's also forced himself on me more than once. I don't feel like God wants me to be in a marriage like that."

Pastor Jim had no words. He was dumbfounded.

"I have never forced myself on you!" Brandon exclaimed.

"Yes, you have! You just don't want anybody to know."

"I really don't know what to say to this. Brandon, I'm in shock at what she's saying. You can't expect her to want to be your wife with you treating her like this." Pastor Jim spoke gently. I saw the disappointment in his eyes. I'm sure he never thought in a million years that Brandon, the golden preacher boy, would behave this way.

After that quick meeting, I felt relieved I had finally spoken up and told someone about what I was going through with him. Everyone in his circle kept saying God brought us together, and that God ordained for us to be married. I couldn't understand where they were getting this information from because God had told me no such thing. I saw the Brandon they did not see, and I wasn't going to let them pressure me into a marriage I knew I would hate and regret.

Brandon was breaking me down. I was already in a vulnerable state from the emotional trauma I had experienced and not gotten over with getting pregnant with Ariel and losing my daddy. No, my daddy had not died, but our relationship had. I was looking for a man to fill that void in my life. Instead of running to my Heavenly Father like I should have in the first place when I was fifteen, I ran away from Him. I ran away from the pain. I buried and blocked out memories and emotions that desperately tried to consume me. I was an emotional mess, which led to me making unwise choices.

I remained in a relationship with a man who did not truly love me. A man who didn't understand me. A man who didn't know how to treat me. A man who could never love me for who I was. A man who betrayed me. A man I couldn't trust with my life. A man I couldn't trust with my daughter. A man who was not true to himself or God. How could he love me when he couldn't be faithful? How could he love me in the right way when he put on a façade about his relationship with God? The ugly truth was he could not! I thought dating a minister would be the best thing for me, but it almost destroyed me! The relationship I had with Brandon robbed me of my peace, self-esteem, joy, some friendships, other relationships, and more than anything it made me feel unworthy of true love.

***

It was also because of this relationship, amongst other things, that I put even more into my relationship with God. My friendship with April sparked my faith walk, but my relationship with Brandon, strengthened it. I didn't understand all of who God was, but this relationship furthered my mission to find out. I grew up in the church. I had been in church every Sunday my whole life, and what I saw, I did not understand.

Is that who God is? I was confused out of my mind. If that was who God was, I wasn't so sure I wanted it. I was watching the people at church. I was listening to what they were saying. I was paying attention to detail. I looked around me and nowhere could I find the answers I was looking for. When I got pregnant with Ariel, I heard the gossip. I was still a child, and I had much to deal with. Church was the one place I thought I would find comfort, but I found just the opposite. Surely this couldn't be who God was. Also, while dating Brandon, I was treated with indifference because of the way I dressed, my tattoo, jewelry, and make-up. Surely this couldn't be who God was either.

It wasn't until much later I learned to separate the two. It wasn't until much later that I realized although they were the people of God, some of them didn't have the heart of God, and they weren't representing Him well. Being so young and still trying to find my way, it was hard learning how to separate the two.

***

To strategically plan my exit from my relationship with Brandon, I started going to his church less and started going back to Peter's Rock more. I was starting to pay attention to the urging in my spirit to focus on my relationship with Jesus more than anything else. I started back going to church every Sunday, not because my mom told me to, but because I wanted to.

I vividly remember a sermon by Elder Henderson. I even remember what I wore that day. I went to church that Sunday feeling burdened down. I was tired of myself. I was tired of Brandon. I was tired of struggling with guilt and feeling shame inside. I went to church that beautiful, sunny day wearing a sleeveless lilac blouse and my favorite floral print lilac skirt. I wore some wedge sandals and a little bit of makeup. My hair was down with a few curls. I looked good if I must say so, on the outside, but inside, I was crying. I put on my best smile and walked through the doors of the church, greeting, and hugging church members as I made my way to my seat.

The praise team and choir sang beautifully during praise and worship. I was filled with emotion; I was about ready to burst. Elder Henderson got up to give his sermon. The sermon was titled "I Come with Baggage." It was like he was preaching directly to me. Throughout the sermon, I was teary-eyed, fighting back the tears, holding them inside. I didn't want anyone to see me.

At the end of the sermon, he called the altar workers and ministers to pray for those who came forward. When he said, "Come," I wanted to get up, but I was glued to my seat.

I felt I needed to go, but something was telling me to stay seated. That was the enemy. I decided to let the Holy Spirit lead me instead. So, instead of sitting there, I stood and slowly started walking forward. As I was walking, I was looking at the ministers to decide who I would go to for prayer, but God said, "No. I want you to come to me." My feet kept moving through my hesitation. I walked past the ministers and missionaries, and I knelt on the altar at the steps to the pulpit. I was broken in spirit; I was in distress. I knelt there and bowed my head. I began silently crying. I was trying to stop, but I couldn't. The silent cry turned into weeping. As I wept, I lowered the rest of my body until my forehead was touching the steps because I didn't want anyone to see my face.

I started quietly praying as I was weeping, *Oh, God, please, forgive me. I need Your help. I need You to heal me. I'll do whatever You want me to do. Please, help me. Please, heal me. Please, forgive me. Please, take away the shame. Please, take away the guilt. I need you. Please, God, I need you. I'm so sorry for everything I've done.* I was pouring out my heart. I was calling out as much as I could.

As I cried, repenting, asking, hoping, and praying for God to hear me, I felt someone touch my back. Then I felt hands on my shoulders, trying to lift me. I didn't know how long I had been there, nor did I care. I just needed a breakthrough. When I looked up, it was my mom. She picked me up, took me into her arms, and held me as I continued crying. She kept whispering in my ear, "Everything is going to be okay."

My mom didn't know I had an emptiness inside literally taking away my ability to live. Mom didn't know I was breathing, sure enough, but I wasn't living. Mom didn't know I was sad. Mom didn't realize how alone I felt. Mom had no idea I was in an emotionally and sometimes physically abusive relationship. I wanted to tell her about my pain, but I didn't think she would understand.

Sorry, I digressed. Back to the point at hand. When the altar workers were done, and we all had gone back to our seats, the praise music started. I danced up and down the aisle of Peter's Rock until I was exhausted. After that service, I felt like a huge weight had been lifted from me. I felt much better. It was like God took that weight to bear it as His own. I decided to stick to God like glue. There was no way I could remain sane without Him. After all, the Bible teaches us, "Ask, and it will be given to you; seek, and you will find; knock, and it will be opened to you (Matt 7:7, NKJV)." I no longer felt like God was mad at me and that He didn't want me. Even after all that I had released, I still had some issues to deal with. Brandon was one of them.

18

I remember an incident when Ariel and I were at home. Brandon had come over around maybe five or six in the evening. I wasn't quite dark yet; it was late summer. I went into my bedroom while Ariel was in her bedroom. He came into my room and closed the door. Instantly, I knew what was on his mind. I didn't like to have sexual encounters when she was home or at the very least when she was awake and walking around. I said, "No, not now. Ariel is awake."

"I don't care; she's not going to come in here," he said sternly, stalking toward me with wickedness in his eyes.

"She might come in here, and I don't want her to see you in here! Get out!" I was afraid.

My words went into one ear and out the other. Then he forced me onto my bed. I was saying, "Stop it," as quietly as I could since I didn't want Ariel to hear. He grabbed at my pants and underwear and yanked them down. He got on his knees to get a better grip; then he forced my legs open. I was trying with all my strength to close them, but he used all his strength to hold them open. Then he started cunnilingus, thinking it would quiet me, but it did not.

Just when I was telling him to stop it yet again, Ariel opened my bedroom door and walked in. I was horrified! I was beyond furious. When he heard Ariel crying, because she was indeed traumatized, he jumped away from me.

I grabbed my clothes, pulled them up, and ran to her. Brandon looked embarrassed and started apologizing. "Get the fuck out!" I yelled at him. He didn't know how to respond to my outburst. He held his head down, apologized again, and then tried to comfort Ariel and me. "Don't touch me; just go."

When he left, I held Ariel close to me while trying to hide my tears. I said, "I'm sorry, baby."

I prayed to God that she wouldn't remember. I felt disgusted. How much longer was I going to let him treat me this way? Something had to change, and it had to change quickly. I couldn't keep going down this road with him. It was wreaking havoc on my life. I asked God to give me the strength to walk away.

The following Sunday after church, we had dinner at my sister Tyra's house. My parents and sisters were there, along with my niece and nephews. I was glad my dad had driven over for some family time. I can't remember how we got on the subject of sexual abuse, but Tyra was certain Ariel was being molested. By who or what I don't know because I never let Ariel out of my sight. It was an absurd suggestion. I wanted to go off on her for being so messy. But I kept my composure, especially since my dad was there.

She drew a picture of a stickman figure and asked Ariel to

Resilient

circle on the picture where she had been touched by a man. I knew the area she would circle; she had just witnessed Brandon being near that part of my body. When she circled the vaginal area, my daddy turned red. He was upset. He said if he ever saw Brandon in West Point or near me and Ariel again, he would be a dead man. I did not doubt that my daddy meant every word.

I wanted to explain to them what happened, but I didn't have the heart to say, "Oh, yeah, Dad, Ariel walked in just when Brandon was about to rape me again, and she's confused by what she saw. She's probably still traumatized from it." I don't think my justification for Ariel's interpretation and confusion would have made him feel better. It would have pissed him off even more.

I looked at my mom with pleading eyes to calm Daddy down. She shook her head in disappointment and said, "You heard your daddy." She was more than pleased to hear my daddy speak on it; she didn't want me with Brandon anymore anyway. Mom knew, without a doubt, I would not defy my father.

"I promise you; I have never left Ariel alone with Brandon or any other man. She is confused. Stop trying to start stuff, Tyra."

"Well, she circled the vaginal area, Robin," Tyra said smugly. "She got it from somewhere." I could have slapped the shit out of her.

I knew exactly where she got it from, but I wasn't about to reveal it. I was too ashamed and embarrassed to do so. Even when I think of the incident today, I cringe. He raped me more than once, but that time was the last. I made every effort not to be alone with him in my apartment or anywhere else.

If I ever needed an additional incentive to get Brandon out of my life, my daddy had given me one. I didn't want to have anything else to do with him. I just had to figure out how to gracefully get out of the relationship.

***

During the spring semester of 2005, I was waiting to hear back from the University of Tennessee College of Pharmacy and the University of Mississippi College of Pharmacy. I'd made a decision the fall of 2004 to give it one more shot. I'd been rejected from Ole Miss twice, but this time, I applied to a second school. My focus was still on being close to my family since I was a single mom, and I didn't want to go too far away from home.

Despite the discouragement I received from Brandon and some I had within, I decided to encourage myself *in the Lord* and apply again. Between 2003 and 2005, while I was attending Mississippi State, I'd also gotten a job as a customer service representative for Gateway 2000, a computer company that thrived in the early 2000's. I worked the night shift, which posed a problem for me when it came to having a sitter for Ariel. My mom was always on my back about working so late. What else was I supposed to do? I needed a job; Gateway paid well. I eventually was able to leave that job and started working at Starkville Children's Clinic. When I was laid off from that job, I worked at Oktibbeha County Hospital as a switchboard operator and with Starkville School District as a substitute teacher. I hated being a substitute! I did not like dealing with other people's children. They were disrespectful. Besides that, it just wasn't what I wanted to do with my life. I'd always wanted to be in the medical field. I remember watching the television show *ER* with my parents every week and wishing I could someday help save lives like that.

Brandon was in education, and he strongly urged me to go into teaching only because that's what he was doing with his life. I wasn't interested in it. But if it meant putting food on my table and providing a roof over our heads, I was willing to give it a try, especially since I had already been rejected from Ole Miss twice.

I was tempted to take a job in Sardis, MS, under an emergency teaching license. I was done with college and needed the money, but I trusted my gut and decided not to. Brandon was upset that I didn't take the job and said I was stupid for turning it down. I could not fathom trying to teach a bunch of high school students about biology and math when I had no teaching experience in the classroom or passion for it.

Working as a substitute teacher made me realize teaching wasn't for me when I told this little girl in eighth grade, "Get your ass out of my classroom!" I said it before I knew it! She was yelling out of the window. I told her to get away from the window and take a seat.

She said, "You need to stay in a child's place, Ms. Terry." I snapped and told her, "Get your ass out of my classroom." Those kids were disrespectful. After that day, I knew deep down in my soul that teaching was not for me. Not getting into pharmacy school was not an option. I didn't know what else I was going to do.

***

Before I sent off my applications for pharmacy school, I put a prayer and a praise over them and left it in God's hands.

I prayed to God, *If You don't do it, Lord, it won't be done. If*

You don't give it to me, Lord, I won't have it. If I don't get into pharmacy school, I don't know what I'm going to do with my life. Teaching other people's kids is not my calling. I love flowers, but I don't have the means to open a flower shop. I want to prove to Ari that we can achieve anything as long as we keep pushing and keep trying. I want to be a mom that she can be proud of. I'm trusting You, God, because I have no other choice than to do so. You know what I need, and only You know where I'm going. Please, let me get into one of these schools, so I can become a pharmacist and prove everybody wrong. So many people counted me out and said I would be nothing because I got pregnant. God, I need You to show Yourself strong. I'm expecting You to come through for me. I'm expecting You to work on my behalf. I trust You because if You don't do it, it won't be done. In Jesus name. Amen.

To my surprise, I was contacted to visit the University of Tennessee for an interview. I was ecstatic and nervous. I told my mom; she was excited for me. When I told my daddy, a man who does not show much emotion, he couldn't hide his smile and pleasure at hearing the news. I even went to see Dr. Fortenberry, my chemistry professor from my days at MUW. I often sought her counsel when I was a student there. I went to her office many days to hang out and talk to her about whatever was on my mind. She was more than a teacher; she was a counselor and a friend. I grew to love her very much, and I wanted to make her proud. Dr. Fortenberry was one of the few people I asked to write a letter of recommendation for me to get into pharmacy school. When I told her about my interview, she was thrilled. She knew how hard I had worked to get there, and she told me that she knew I would do great. I got advice from her about what I should wear and how I should style my hair.

She advised me to style my hair straightened, wear a black or navy-blue pantsuit, and low-heeled shoes. I did everything she instructed me to do.

***

I didn't tell Brandon about my interview. I didn't want any negative energy around me and what I was praying for God to do. Getting into pharmacy school was a definite way of escape to get out of the relationship with him. I would be miles away, and there was no way he would move to Memphis.

I drove to Memphis the day before my interview. Mom was a nervous wreck. She didn't want me to go alone, but I said I would be fine. I printed the directions from the internet and was going to make the drive early enough, so I wouldn't be on the road at night. My dad made sure my SUV was ready for the road, and I was on my way. When I checked into my hotel, I called my parents and April to let them know I made it safely. I talked to April for a while that evening. We went over interview questions; she offered words of encouragement saying, "God has already worked it out. I believe you will get in. You have to go in and be yourself."

The next day, I arrived for my interview fifteen minutes early. I was anxious and nervous. I sat and waited, tapping the heel of my foot with the feeling of uncertainty and fear I couldn't shake. My stomach was queasy, and my heart was fluttering. My throat was dry, and I felt light-headed. That's just how nervous I was. I whispered, "Lord, help me. Calm me down; I know it's already done." I saw people going in and out of the interview rooms, looking just as nervous as I was. Some of them, however, looked conceited and overly confident.

When my name was called, I was led to a room, where I met Dr. Rawls, my soon to be professor, and a student from the admissions committee. I firmly shook both of their hands, smiled, and then Dr. Rawls offered me a seat. I sat down, and the interview began. I was asked the typical interview questions; then he asked something I'll never forget.

"What is the most difficult thing you've ever done, and how did you accomplish it?"

I could do one of two things. I could ramble off some gibberish, or I could be honest. I could let my guard down just a little bit to give them a peek into my life, so they will know the real me, not what I think they want to see.

"The most difficult thing I've ever had to do was graduate high school, and then attend college with a child. I got pregnant with my daughter, Ariel, when I was fifteen. It was hard navigating through high school, especially in a small town. My pregnancy was the latest gossip for a while, and it was discouraging. I wanted to give up many times."

"Wow!" Dr. Rawls said in surprise. The student sitting next to him looked at me with amazement while nodding her head in agreement. "What would you say was the reason you kept going?"

"My mom was my biggest cheerleader. She encouraged me a lot. When she wasn't offering support and encouragement, I learned how to do it for myself. I also wanted to be a mother my daughter could be proud of. I want her to be able to look at me and feel like she has the strongest mom in the world. God saw me through it."

"I think you have a wonderful story, Robin. It could help a

lot of people someday. I'm glad to see what you've accomplished so far." Dr. Rawls looked at me with pride. It felt almost like I was his daughter, and he was proud of me.

After that discussion, we talked about a few more things, and before I knew it, the interview was over. After the interview, we toured the campus and visited a student's apartment to get an idea of living in Memphis. I met a couple of other hopeful pharmacy students that day. I was excited about my future; still hoping and praying God would open the door for me to get in. I left my interview feeling hopeful and invigorated. I felt even if God didn't open this door, He had something better for me. I just wished I knew what it was.

19

After returning home from my interview, I did not attempt to contact Brandon. I had already started calling him less and making less time for him before I left. I no longer wanted him to be a part of our lives. I was sick and tired of being tired. I wanted to take what energy I had left to focus on creating a better life for my daughter and me. I had been praying for God to create a way of escape to get out of the relationship. Brandon had shown some possessive and fearsome characteristics throughout our relationship. I didn't know if he would try to hurt me or not, but I didn't want to risk it. He had made several statements before saying he would never let me go. He'd also said he loved me to death, and he wasn't going to live without me. When he made those statements, it was the look in his eyes that scared me the most.

I decided instead of staying in a relationship out of fear of being physically hurt that I would pray and strategically create distance to slowly get him out of my life. My prayer was, *Lord, before he hurts me or kills me, kill him.* I didn't want him to die, but

I didn't want him to hurt me either. I didn't know what else to pray. It probably wasn't the right thing to ask of God, but that's all I had. That's what I held on to when I prayed to God to get me out of that relationship. If He had to choose who was going to live, I needed God to choose me over Brandon.

"How was your trip to Memphis?" Brandon asked over the phone shortly after I returned home. He'd called me; I'm assuming because I hadn't called him in a few days.

"How do you know I was in Memphis?"

"Somebody I know told me they saw you there. They saw you checking into Holiday Inn."

"Who saw me?"

"Don't worry about all that. It's somebody I know."

"Memphis was fine."

"What were you doing there?"

"Why?"

"Because I want to know. So, what were you doing there?"

"If you must know, I had an interview for pharmacy school."

"Why didn't you tell me about it?"

"Because I didn't."

"Well, why? You didn't want me to go with you?"

"No, I didn't want you to go. I wanted to be alone."

"Well, how was it?"

"It was fine. I think I did all right."

"Okay, let me know if you get in."

I was horrified! How did he know I had gone to Memphis? When I checked into that hotel, I was the only person in the lobby. I didn't see anyone who looked familiar. Brandon didn't have a lot of friends, at least not any friends I had met. I felt uneasy about it.

Had he followed me? Did he somehow manage to put a tracker on my car? Surely, not. Either way, I didn't like it. I wasn't comfortable knowing he knew where I was without me telling him.

Sometime later, I found out I had been accepted into pharmacy school. I couldn't believe it. I mean, I knew it was happening, but it was surreal. I just kept saying, "Thank you, Jesus!" over and over. God had proven Himself to me again! I held on to my faith, and He made sure I wasn't holding on to it in vain. When I ended the call with the pharmacy department's secretary, Ms. Wanda, I hopped in my truck and drove to the hospital, where my mom worked. I could barely contain myself. I practically ran through the doors of the emergency room to see her.

"Mama, guess what?"

"What is it?" she asked nervously. She thought something bad had happened.

"I got in!" I squealed.

"What?"

"I got in pharmacy school at UT!" I said, jumping up and down, clapping my hands in excitement.

Mama was speechless for a second. Then she grabbed and hugged me tightly, crying, telling me she was so proud of me.

She let me go and started telling everybody in the department that I was going to pharmacy school. Her co-workers knew I had gotten pregnant in high school, and the comments weren't always positive. Mama now had bragging rights.

Next, I told Daddy and April. They were happy for me. I don't think I had ever seen my dad so proud. I wasn't worried about not succeeding because I loved school, and even more than that, I knew God had my back. If I got in, I knew I would graduate on time without failing a single class.

***

I eventually got around to telling Brandon. I didn't call him to tell him. I waited for him to call me, and he soon did. He wanted to know if I had found out whether or not I got into pharmacy school. I told him I had gotten in.

Eventually, he convinced me to go out to lunch with him one day. I met up with Brandon in Tupelo, a city about an hour from West Point, for lunch. Before going to eat, he asked me to get in his car so that we could go for a ride. I was hesitant, but I agreed to ride with him. He took me to a car lot in Tupelo.

"Why are we here?" I asked.

"To look at cars. Which one do you want?"

"I have something to drive. I don't need another one. There is nothing wrong with the vehicle I'm driving."

"It's older, and you are going to need something dependable to get up and down the road in."

"My SUV is dependable."

"Just get out and look at one," he said with a crooked smile. "You'll love it."

He opened his door to get out. He walked around to my door to let me out. He walked me over to a burgundy Chrysler PT Cruiser. It was nice. I was currently driving my mom's old Mercury Mountaineer. I can't deny I wanted a newer vehicle, but what I was driving was just fine. It had no mechanical problems. Pretty soon, a salesman was outside, and I was test driving the car.

As soon as I started driving it, I knew I wanted that car. But

Resilient

at what cost? Even if I never paid one car note, I knew getting that car would cost me something. I had a decision to make as I was going through different scenarios in my head while driving down Gloster Street.

I tuned out the salesman as he talked to Brandon. I wasn't interested in anything they were saying. I drove the car with a smile while repulsed inside at the fact that he was trying to buy me. The fact of the matter was that I wasn't for sale. Neither was my daughter.

As I drove, I consulted with God. *Lord, what shall I do? Do I take this car now and neglect what I want? It's time for me to consider me, not him. Lord, what do I do?*

I felt this hard, "No!" drop in my spirit. An uneasy feeling of dread came over me; I knew the Holy Spirit was telling me to go the other way. Instead of being disobedient this time, I followed what I knew in my heart God was telling me to do.

After we got back to the car lot, Brandon was sure I was going to say I wanted the car. I smiled and said, "This is a really nice car, but I don't want it."

His face dropped. There was nothing he could say to make me take it. We got back in his car, and he drove me back to my vehicle. He asked me to meet him at a local restaurant, and I agreed. I don't remember much of what we talked about, but I do remember drinking a lot of sweet tea, one of my favorite drinks, which prompted my bladder to send me to the restroom.

When I returned from the restroom, I looked into my purse for lotion to moisturize my dry hands. While searching for my lotion, I saw a velvet box. It jumped out at me. I paused for a moment and then picked it up. I looked at Brandon and asked, "What is this?"

"Open it!" he said with a smile but with uncertainty in his eyes.

I opened the box. I could not believe my eyes. I was staring at the most beautiful ring I had ever seen. It was perfect! It was exactly what I would have picked out myself. I opened my mouth to speak, but not a single word came out. *You have got to be kidding me! After all this time and all the bullshit, he's going to ask me to marry him again?*

"This is the ring I should have gotten you the first time," he said. "I want a fresh start. Will you marry me?"

20

I looked at him, and I saw how sincere he was. But my heart wasn't in it anymore; it hadn't been for a long time. I wanted a fresh start, too, and I wanted it without him. For once, I was considering what I wanted and not what anyone else expected of me. I didn't want to hurt him, but not hurting him meant hurting me. I didn't want to hurt me anymore.

Before I could speak, I started shaking my head, "No, I can't."

"Why not?"

"I don't want to get married anymore. I just need to be alone. I need to focus on school and Ariel."

"What about Ariel? She needs a father in her life."

"I know, and my dad is the man who is fathering her right now, and he always will," I said confidently. No matter what my relationship with my father was, I knew he would always be there for Ariel. She was his "Boojack," and she always would be.

I gave him the ring back. As he took the box from my hands,

I noticed how sad and disappointed he was. I wasn't going to let his feelings get in the way of my happiness. I was ready and willing to face my future without fear and without him. We didn't have much to talk about after the proposal, so he paid the check, and we left the restaurant. Before I got in my vehicle, I told him I'd talk to him later. I drove back home, telling myself over and over that I had made the right decision. Besides, there was no way I could go home and tell my father I had agreed to marry Brandon after all that had transpired between us. I don't believe anyone in my family would have approved, not that I needed their approval, anyway. I made the decision based solely on believing God had someone better for me. Someone who wouldn't hurt, belittle, betray, or mistreat me. The Bible says God wants us to have a life in abundance (John 10:10 HCSB) not defeat. The entire time I was in a relationship with Brandon, all I felt was defeat. I was done. I was ready to move on.

After the proposal and buying a new car didn't work to keep me in his life, Brandon brought up Ariel. He literally tried to convince me to leave Ariel with him while I attended pharmacy school. When I stated there was no way in hell I would leave my child in his custody, he dared to get upset. I have several reasons for not wanting to leave my daughter with him. I'll give you two of them. The first reason was that he wasn't her father. I never trusted any man around my daughter without being present. Trust is something that must be earned; it is not freely given. It was my job to protect Ariel at all costs. Leaving her with someone other than her father, wasn't an option. She barely saw her father anyway, and I didn't trust in him one hundred percent of the time to keep her safe. It's not like he was reliable. So, if I barely trusted her to be in the care of her biological father, what made Brandon think I would trust him to take care of her?

Brandon tried to say everything he could think of to convince me to leave her with him. He said that since he was in education, he would make sure she got her schoolwork done and she'd be properly educated. He also said my parents would not be able to care for her the way he could because they were separated. He went on and on with his fake tears and concerns, trying to persuade me to let him keep Ariel. I don't know what he was thinking, but I wasn't going for that.

The second reason I dared not leave my daughter with Brandon was that I was annoyed by a previous incident. Brandon had come over to my apartment. He sat at the desk I had my computer on. Ariel had just come from her room, and he gestured for her to come to him. When she walked over to Brandon, he picked her up, placed her on his left leg, and put his arm around her to hold her up. It seemed innocent enough. Then, he did something repulsive. While she was sitting there, he started gently caressing her thigh with his left hand.

My instincts flared, and a red flag went up. I didn't like that. I immediately told Ariel, "Get up. Go to your room and play with your toys." I questioned Brandon about what he was doing, and he got offensive. "Why were you rubbing Ariel's thigh?" He didn't see anything wrong with what he was doing. I said, "That is inappropriate behavior. I have a father, and he's never in my life rubbed my thigh or any part of my body."

Brandon jumped from the chair, trying to defend himself, but I wasn't having it. "You better not ever in your life touch her in that way or any other way again." He left my apartment pissed off that day, but I had no regard for his thoughts or feelings.

After he left, I called April and told her what had happened. I asked her if I overreacted. She wholeheartedly agreed with me! That was all the confirmation I needed. April and I had heard rumors about him fooling around with teenage girls before. Of course, none of these rumors were validated, but I wasn't going to risk it. My daughter was going to grow up to become a young lady, and beyond a shadow of a doubt, I would be in jail for pulling a Lorena Bobbitt on him or any other man for thinking he could get away with hurting Ariel.

I never told my family about any of the things I was dealing with concerning Brandon. I never told anyone except April, and half of the time, I didn't tell her until after a significant amount of time had passed. I was too ashamed. I was most ashamed at the fact that I was still in a relationship with this man. I ignored sign after sign that he was not right for me, but the one sign I could not ignore was the lack of trust I had in him when it came to Ariel. Seeing him rubbing her thigh, I think, was God's way of giving me another sign I needed to get the hell away from that man. I knew it was just a matter of time. Like I said earlier, I was afraid for a while from the things he said and the look of pure evil in his eyes, but God helped me. I overcame that fear and did what I had to do.

***

By August, it was time to leave and head to Memphis to start pharmacy school. I was nervous and praying I wouldn't fail. It was going to be my first time away from home with no family, and more importantly, it would be my first time without my baby girl. I was sad, very sad. I let my parents, particularly my mom, convince me to leave Ariel with them so that I could focus on school. But I didn't want to leave her. Since I'd given birth, it had always been Ariel and me. I finished high school with her, started and finished college with her, worked two jobs at a time with her, laughed with her, cried with her, had fun with her, went through frustration with her, faced the good, the bad, and the ugly with her. I grew up with her. She was my everything. I didn't want her to grow up hating me for leaving her, believing I had abandoned her and went on to live my life without her. Austin was already not in her life like he should have been, and I didn't want her thinking I had deserted her, too.

I had many mixed emotions during my preparations to leave home. I had finished up my unfinished business with Brandon and was looking forward to my newfound freedom. To that case and point, I was optimistic. On the other hand, I was nervous about my future; I had no idea what was ahead. The only thing I was certain of was that I was taking God with me, and I was hoping for the best.

I remember the day I left home. I moved my furniture into storage; I had decided to live in on-campus housing until I got a feel for the area. When it was time for me to leave, my mom started cleaning up the house. She was sweeping and dusting to keep herself busy. Ariel was following me all over the house and outside while I was packing up the truck. My heart was heavy. I was dreading leaving her there.

Before leaving, I walked back into the house one last time. I was looking for my dad to tell him I was about to go, but I couldn't find him anywhere. I guess he didn't want to see his baby girl leave, either. I hugged Ariel tightly, and said, "I loved you. Mommy isn't leaving you forever. I'm just going to school, but I'm going to come home every weekend to see you, and I'll call you all the time."

That was a promise I was going to surely keep. Ariel started crying; she didn't want me to leave. A couple of tears fell from my eyes. I quickly dried them to keep from losing my composure in front of her. I tried to hug my mom goodbye, but she shoved me out of the house while trying to hide her tears.

My voice was cracking as I said, "Ariel, I'll call you when I make it. I'll see you on Friday!"

Then, I turned on my heels and left. I didn't look back. If I had, I wouldn't have left. When I got in the truck, out of the corner of my eye, I saw Ariel standing at the screen door crying. I dared not look directly at her because I wouldn't have been able to leave. My biggest regret out of all the terrible decisions I made was leaving her with my parents. I should have gone with my first mind to take her with me so that we could conquer another goal together. I was too young and afraid, so I listened to my parents. To this day, I wish I hadn't.

God's Glory

God was so good to me, and He was with me the entire time I was going through so many changes. He was there as I faced adversity from forces within and out of my control. Looking back, even when I couldn't trace Him, I can see how He was there. He was there in the girl who gave me money when I had less than $1 in the bank. He was there when I considered becoming a stripper to take care of Ariel, yet He created a way of escape. He was there in the furniture store when I paid with a check they never cashed. He was there in my job search when job opportunities landed in my lap, and I got paid more than minimum wage every time. He was there in the "I just want to check on you" phone calls I got from April. He was there in the hugs and words of encouragement I received from my mother. He was there every time Ariel wiped tears from my eyes. I couldn't see it back then because I was blinded by everything I was dealing with.

Everything I went through worked out for my good. I learned a lot. I learned that we have to be willing to give up something for God to give us something. I had to open my hands and heart to let go of unforgiveness for God to move in my life in a mighty way. Some of us don't understand we have to be willing to open our hearts and give ourselves away, to give away everything burdening us to God for Him to give us Himself. We have to wake up every day willing to give God our issues in exchange for His peace and joy. We have got to learn to let go, and that is something I learned during this time of my life.

I forgave myself. I forgave my dad. I forgave Austin. I forgave Brandon. I was also finally able to be at peace with being a teenage mother. I was listening to William Murphy's *All Day* album released in 2004 before it went mainstream. There is a track on that album titled *'I Know Why I am Here.'* On that track, William Murphy gives his testimony about how he was born to teenage parents. He said he was called a mistake because he was a result of his parents' sin. He said, "I came here to tell some teenage mama tonight that your baby is not a mistake. The devil did not make you pregnant. The devil cannot give life. God's got a plan for your life. I'm not a mistake. I was on the mind of God when my daddy met my mama! I was in the plan of God when my daddy met my mama!" When I heard this track, I cried and repented before The Lord. I had been wrong! It was through this song that God showed me that Ariel wasn't a mistake; My life wasn't over and doomed to failure. God still had a plan for us. I was finally at peace with what had transpired because of my decision that Friday night.

    I let go of my fear. I let go of my old way of thinking. I chose to wake up every day to work on being a better me. It was through prayer, fasting, persistence, and pressing that I was able to do this. It didn't happen overnight. Because I forgave my daddy, I was comfortable with him again. That was all that mattered to me. I love my daddy so much, and the distance between the two of us hurt me more than anything. I was just glad to have my daddy back. I was his little girl again, and that made all the difference in my life. I didn't hold a grudge against anyone. I just wanted to live. I wanted to be happy.

    I also learned to trust and depend on God completely and wholeheartedly. I had to trust that He knew better than me. Over time, I learned to yield my will for His will. I asked God to come into my heart to mold and transform me into the person He wanted me to be. I'm not saying I stopped making mistakes because I still made more, but I did learn in the making of my mistakes that God is not One to force us to do anything. He's given all of us free will. The Holy Spirit guides us, but it is up to us to take heed to what He is showing us.

What helped me the most when it came to building a relationship with God was that even while I was making my mistakes, He never left me. He was always constant. He always made it work out for my good. It wasn't comfortable or easy. That's why it is always best to go with His plan and not our own. I could have avoided a lot of heartache and pain if I had gone with the leading of the Holy Spirit. My mistakes caused me to trust God more. My mistakes forced me to have faith that everything would get better. But I had to be willing to yield. I had to be willing to believe. I had to be willing to trust. Finally, I had to be bold in my asking and patient in my waiting.

The one thing I didn't do during this time that I should have was deal with my pain. I was still holding on to hurt I couldn't seem to let go of because I'd buried it, and I wasn't ready to process it. I never brought it up. Perhaps I held on to it as a reminder not to let people get too close to me. If they can't get close to me, then they can't hurt me. I didn't want to deal with it, so I slapped a Band-Aid on it and kept it moving. I was still fragile. That's one thing I couldn't lie to myself about. I said, "Lord, we will deal with this later." I needed to keep my focus on succeeding in pharmacy school and taking care of Ariel. God kept me strong, and for that, I was grateful.

Resilient through Deception...

21

Once I officially started pharmacy school, I was on cloud nine. The first week of school left me feeling optimistic. I met some great people. My roommates were nice, and we got along well. My room was small with concrete walls, a small built-in desk, a sink, and a twin-sized bed. There was also a small wooden chest with 3 drawers for storing clothing and a wooden wardrobe for hanging clothes. I placed a television on top of the chest. I put my computer on the desk. Every morning, I watched Joyce Meyer before going to class. While I was away from my room, I left gospel music playing from my computer throughout the day. It was like I was an eighteen-year-old freshman in college again, trying to feel people out, deciphering the good from the bad. There were some people I connected with, and some I didn't.

A couple of weeks into pharmacy school, I met a charismatic young man in his third year of pharmacy school that I'll call Kent. I met him when I went out to a club with a couple of my classmates. I wasn't into the club scene, but I didn't want to come off as antisocial. So, when I was invited, I decided to socialize. I felt it was a bad idea, but I went anyway. There were a couple of reasons why I didn't want to go. One reason was that I had vowed to stay out of the clubs. I had outgrown that part of my life, and I didn't like being there anymore. The second reason was that I didn't have any clubbing clothes! I no longer wore short skirts and tank tops. As I grew in my faith, I no longer wanted the negative attention I received from dressing like that. After going through my clothes, I decided on wearing a long skirt with a matching blouse—definitely not club clothes!

I had no idea Kent was going to be there. I thought it was going to be a girls' night. When we got inside, I wasn't in the mood. I sat down the whole night, watching them have a great time. I wanted to be in my room watching TV. Kent asked me to hold his jacket while he danced. I didn't have a problem with that; it wasn't like I was having the time of my life. If I had driven myself, I would have left. But my ride home was on the dance floor, having a good time.

We got back in late that night. While I was getting ready for bed, I received a call from an unknown number. I answered, and it was Kent. He asked if I had seen his driver's license because he couldn't find it. He said it was in his jacket. I said I hadn't seen it, and we ended the call. *Who gave him my number? I bet he didn't even lose his driver's license. He just wanted my number to call me.*

He called me again the next day and asked if I knew where the closest Wal-Mart was. I said I'd heard about the Wal-Mart in West Memphis, Arkansas, being close. Long story short, we ended up going to Wal-Mart together. As we walked through Wal-Mart looking for snacks, we asked general personal questions like, "Where are you from?" You know the usual, but I distinctly remember asking him, "How old are you?"

He shared his age. Because he was nearly thirty, I decided to ask him more personal questions like, "Are you dating? Do you have children?"

The answer was, "No," to those questions. He didn't hesitate to respond to any of my inquiries, but his eyes shifted. He didn't look at me when he answered. Something didn't feel right in my spirit, but I ignored it because I liked him. It was music to my ears. I thought he was cute. Truth was, I was just out of an abusive relationship, and I didn't need to start a new one. I didn't have a desire to be in a relationship, but I did want someone to hang out and have some fun with. So, I decided to save his number in my phone, and the rest was history.

Another young man came into my life shortly after starting pharmacy school. He was my classmate. His name was Cedric. Cedric reminded me of Reuben Studdard. He was sweet, fun, and a ray of sunshine in my life. I could talk to him about anything. Cedric and I started spending a lot of time together in January of 2006. Other than April, he had become my best friend. As time went on, Kent and I spent more and more time together. We made sure we saw each other, especially on Fridays because I would leave to head home to see Ariel for the weekend. I wouldn't say we were in a relationship. We never defined it, but I did like him a lot.

About a month into our friendship, I asked my friend, Sammie, (another important person in my life from pharmacy school) about Kent since they were from the same hometown. Sam and I were studying one night at the General Education Building, and I brought it up. Sam was vague with me. He didn't answer any of my questions directly. He quizzically asked me, "What did he tell you?"

"He said he's never been married. He's not in a relationship, and he doesn't have any children."

"What else?"

"That's about it. We've been hanging out a lot."

"Do you like him?"

"Yeah, I do. "

"Well, I suggest you ask Bunny about him then."

"I'm asking you, though. Is there something he's not telling me?"

"Just talk to Bunny."

Bunny is one of my line sisters. She's from the same hometown as Sam and Kent. I should have called her right away, but I didn't. I pushed what he said to the back of my mind and continued to study.

I did pray about Kent. I asked God to give me a sign as to whether or not I should continue being friends with him. What happened to me next was bizarre. I went to sleep. I slept just fine. When I rose the next morning to use the restroom, my urine was all blood. I was flooded with fear. I didn't know what was going on. I checked to make sure it wasn't my period. My period wasn't due for another couple of weeks. *Maybe it's just a one-time thing.*

When I went to use the restroom again later that morning, the same thing happened. I did the only thing I could think of; I called my mom and told her what was going on. She told me to drive home that day to see a doctor. The good thing was that it was a

Resilient

Friday morning. I was going home anyway, so I wouldn't miss class.

Once I arrived home, I drove to the emergency room where my mom was still working, and the doctor ran some tests. He couldn't find anything wrong with my kidneys, blood count, or bladder. He said it was a mystery to him! It was a mystery to all of us! He prescribed some medicine for a urinary tract infection and said if I wasn't better within a week, I would need to see a urologist. *Maybe this is the sign from God I've been looking for. Maybe it's a warning to not go down this road with Kent.* But what did my hard-headed behind continue to do? I kept spending time with Kent. God soon sent me another warning.

A few weeks later, I started having a little bit of pain in my butt cheek. There was a lump there. The pain got so bad that I went to the student clinic to get it checked out. The doctor took one look and said, "You need to go to the emergency room to have it lanced. This is a boil, and it's too big for me to handle in the clinic."

I went to the emergency room at the university hospital downtown. The wait was taking forever. I called my mom; she said to come home. This time, I had to miss class because it occurred in the middle of the week.

I drove straight to the emergency room. I got there before the end of my mom's shift. Dr. Henry once again took care of me. He lanced and drained the boil. It was the worst pain I had ever felt in my life. Yes, it hurt worse than giving birth. I cried, asking God why all of this was happening to me, I'm pretty sure that was another warning, but I kept hanging out with Kent. I ignored all the signs. I ignored all of the red flags. I ignored my instincts that kept telling me to end things with him. It felt like he was seeing other people, but I didn't have proof. Because we had never defined our relationship, I tried not to read too much into it. It's not like I was in love. I cared about him and enjoyed our time together. We had already had sex, and I didn't want to drop him yet. Besides, it was more than just sex. We were friends. He cooked for me. We watched movies together, went out for long walks together, kissed, hugged, and laughed together. Whatever it was that Kent was doing on the side, he had enough respect for me not to do it in my face. When we were together, we were together; and when we were not together, we weren't.

I had been through so much with Brandon I didn't want to define anything, anyway. Cedric and Sam used to joke with me about being in love, but I kept telling them I wasn't. I had no interest whatsoever in love.

My relationship with Kent changed in a way that crushed me in December of 2005. I found out I was pregnant. Again, I wasn't consistent with my birth control. I was not happy about it. It screwed up my plans. When I told Kent about my pregnancy, he promptly said, "I want you to have an abortion. We haven't been together long enough for you to be having my baby," he spat.

"I know that, but I've had an abortion before. I am not doing it again. That is something I will never live through again! It was hard enough the first time."

"If the dude you had the abortion for the first time didn't want the baby, what makes you think I want a baby?" He was so cruel.

"I'm not having an abortion whether you agree with it or not. You don't have to be there for this baby. I can do it by myself if I have to."

With that, the conversation ended. I left. I didn't talk to him

Resilient

for a few days afterward. The following weekend, I had to head home for winter break. I'm not sure when he left because I hadn't talked to him. I tried calling him after I got home, and he didn't answer. He ignored every phone call. Then I remembered what Sam told me a while back. He'd told me to ask Bunny about him, so I called my line sister. I asked her if she knew Kent. She did know him; she knew a lot about his life. Bunny began by telling me that he had a fiancée and three other children. He had been with the mother of his children since high school. She told me she was going to drive past his mom's house. We ended our call. Then she called me back about half-an-hour later, saying she drove past his mom's house and saw his truck there. His fiancée and kids were there as well.

    I couldn't believe what I was hearing. I was crushed, not because I was in love because I wasn't; I was hurt because this man had repeatedly lied to me. He had denied his whole family, his entire truth, just to get some ass. We were supposed to be friends. I felt in my spirit something wasn't right; I ignored it all. Now the cat was out of the bag, and I was angry. He was also treating me coldly. I cared about him. I thought he cared about me, but his actions proved he only cared about himself.

    After I got off the phone with Bunny the second time, I sent Kent a nasty text message. I specifically remember typing, "Nigga, you ain't shit!" I was beyond angry. I'd told my mom I was pregnant and what was going on. Her first question was, "Are you going to keep the baby?"

    I said, "Yes, I'm going to keep the baby."

    My mom always had a way of calming me down. She said, "Let Kent be. Everything is going to be all right. You don't have to worry about how you're going to take care of the baby. There's no way your dad and I would let the baby go without anything."

Of course, I knew this was true from my previous experiences with Ariel. Mom said, "Every dog has his day, and his day is coming."

I believed her. I went downstairs and cried. I got all of my tears out. Then I did what I knew how to do best ... I sucked it up. I decided that for the time being, I would stop focusing on what was going on with Kent and enjoy the Christmas break with my family.

In January, it was time to return to class. I attended a social event for pharmacy students. Cedric and Sam were there, as well as my roommate, Jessica. We all rode together in the same car. While at the event, Kent and I started texting each other. I'm pretty sure I initiated the messaging, but I don't remember why. I can't say word for word what was said, but the gist of the messages was he didn't want to have anything to do with the baby or me. All I wanted was for him to acknowledge my feelings and show some compassion, but there was none. I was trying to keep it together at the event; I couldn't. I started crying; the tears wouldn't stop falling. Cedric and Sam were pissed. I remember they started talking shit about him. Then they told me to grab my stuff so we could leave. I sat in the back seat and cried until I got back to campus. They said to stay away from Kent and not say anything else to him.

I didn't listen, though. To get Kent to talk to me, I eventually sent him a text stating I was going to get an abortion. Yeah, so I lied. He called me later that day. I didn't answer, but I did call him back. I should have listened to my mom, Cedric, and Sam. I shouldn't have given him the time of day. I shouldn't have spoken his name.

By the end of January, we were on speaking terms again. Of

course, he wanted to know if I had made my appointment for an abortion. I lied by saying I had made one, and it was coming soon. One night, we decided to get together to hang out for a while. Yes, I know it was a dumb decision, but I went anyway. We lived in on-campus housing. I was upstairs, and he was downstairs. I walked downstairs to the apartment he shared with his three roommates. He opened the door, wearing a muscle shirt and shorts.

    We had food, watched movies, laughed, and talked for a little while. He started kissing me and ultimately, we had sex. When we were done, he asked if I was thirsty. Kent said he had some juice, fruit punch to be exact, and offered me a drink. He placed the cup on the countertop, next to the sink. He removed the juice from the refrigerator. As he fixed my drink, he had his back turned to me with the cup and carton of juice directly in front of him. It took him longer than it should have to pour the juice, and I couldn't see what he was doing. He put the juice back in the fridge, then turned to give me the cup. I took a sip to taste it. It wasn't smooth like juice should be; it was gritty.

    "What's with your juice?" I asked. "It's gritty."

    "Oh, that's just the way they make it. It always tastes like this," he said, looking away from me. I'd never had that brand before, so I went on his word.

    My gut feeling told me not to drink it, but I was thirsty. He drank some as well, so I didn't think any more of it. I fell asleep shortly after. I awakened with a jolt to find him sitting at his desk, studying. I felt weird. It was like everything was hazy. I asked him, "What time is it?"

    He said it was after 11:00 p.m., so I decided to head back up to my room. I went back to sleep when I got to my room, but I woke up again. This time, I felt something weird going on in my lower abdomen. I had to use the bathroom. After I finished, I saw a blood clot in the toilet. I called Kent and explained that I thought I was having a miscarriage. He was calm and alert, almost as if he had been waiting for me to call.

Kent drove me to one of the metro hospitals that have quality maternity care. I wore sweatpants, a t-shirt, and a pair of sneakers. We didn't talk to each other on the ride over. I kept going over everything that had happened in the past twenty-four hours in my head. I remember thinking, *What did he put in my drink?* That thought kept spinning on its axis, going around and around in my mind. I had so much head noise. *Did he give me something to cause this miscarriage? I should have listened to my mom and stayed away from him. Why is this happening to me? I bet Kent is happy about this. He didn't want me to have the baby anyway.*

Various thoughts were consuming me, and there was nothing I could do about it. I sat there thinking, dazed, and wishing I was not going through this. *God, maybe it's for the best. This man is nothing like I thought, anyway. He's selfish and inconsiderate, not to mention a liar. He only thinks of himself.*

When we got to the emergency room, I signed in and told the receptionist I thought I was having a miscarriage. It wasn't long before I was called back to triage and put into a room. I think I made my nurse, a young African American female with a spunky haircut, nervous because while she was drawing my blood, she asked me if I knew what my blood type was.

"Blood type. What's that?" I asked with a smile. Clearly, I knew what blood type meant; after all, I was a pharmacy student. Better yet, I knew what my blood type was from giving birth to

Ariel. But there was a disconnect between my psyche and my thought process. I couldn't think straight, so I started laughing. The nurse gave me the side-eye with a slight frown and said, "Okay, the doctor will probably just give you a Rhogam shot." Then she hastily walked out of the room. I looked to my left at Kent and stopped laughing while tears started streaming.

"Are you all right?" he asked with a puzzled expression. "You're not acting like your normal self."

I inhaled sharply, "I'm fine. You don't have to pretend to care. I bet you're happy about this, anyway." I stared at him; then looked away when he didn't have a response. We waited in silence until the nurse came back into the room. She said I needed to go to ultrasound, and someone would be there to get me shortly. When I got to the ultrasound room, I pulled my pants down below my waist and lay back on the bed as I was instructed to do. The ultrasound technician lifted my shirt and put some jelly on my abdomen and began spreading it around with the wand.

After she had taken a few pictures, I asked if my baby was still alive. "I'm not allowed to answer that question for you, ma'am. The doctor has to give you that information," she said with a saddened expression. I knew what the answer to my question was at that moment. I silently cried as I accepted my baby's fate.

When the ultrasound was complete, the orderly came back to take me to my room in the emergency department. Kent was still in the room, waiting for me. I sat back on the bed and waited for the doctor to come in. I didn't have anything to say to Kent, and I'm sure he had no idea what to say to me. So, we waited in deafening silence. The doctor, Dr. Frankenstein, and the nurse came into the room. Dr. Frankenstein was tall with blonde hair. He had a terrible demeanor and bedside manner. Dr. Frankenstein confirmed I had miscarried the baby.

"So, all of the tissue is gone?" I asked because I was between twelve and fourteen weeks pregnant, at least I think I was. I actually can't remember exactly how far along I was in the pregnancy. I vividly remember the day I miscarried.

"Yes, it is," he said in a condescending tone. He didn't even give me a second glance. He was as cold as Kent was. Besides, how can all of the tissue be gone when I'd only seen a couple of blood clots? He talked to me like I was stupid, like I didn't know any better. The doctor left the room; then, the nurse administered the Rhogam shot.

Afterward, I was discharged to go home. The ride back to campus was much quicker than the ride to the hospital. I was still quiet with nothing to say to Kent. He asked if I was hungry. It was after midnight. I didn't have an appetite, but I agreed to get something to eat because he kept pressing me about it like he gave a damn. We drove through the drive-thru of some fast food restaurant and headed back to campus. After he parked his SUV, I hopped out and headed back up to my room.

"Are you going to be all right?"

"I'm fine," I said firmly and walked away without another word. I didn't bother to look back. I walked with my head held down, trying to reel in my emotions, trying to take in what the hell just happened to me, and why in the hell it was happening. *That's what I get for being hardheaded.*

22

Around 7:30 a.m., I got up to get ready for class. I was going to be late, but I needed to go. My roommates had already left. I needed to take a shower to wake up and start the day anew and refreshed. I got my stuff together and headed to the bathroom. When I got into the shower, I felt pressure between my legs like something was about to fall out my vagina. As I stood there, blood started to run down my legs. In an instant, there was splatter. I heard a soft thud hit the bottom of the tub. I thought it was just another blood clot, but when I looked down, what I saw almost made me lose my mind.

There it was, part of my placenta, and my baby laying there in the tub as the water from my shower rinsed the blood down the drain. I turned my shower off and stood there in shock. I couldn't move. My heart crumbled; I started wailing. When I muscled up the courage to move, I wrapped a towel around myself, went back to my room, grabbed my phone, and called my mom.

"Hello," her voice was soothing, but I couldn't speak. I was crying uncontrollably.

"Robin! What's wrong, baby?" she was instantly worried about me.

"The baby. I just lost the baby. It came out while I was in the shower," I sobbed. "The placenta did, too."

"Where are you now?"

"I'm in my room."

"Are you alone?"

"Yes, ma'am," I cried. I could barely get my words out.

"Listen to me carefully. Do exactly as I say." Mom was calm and in nurse/mommy mode.

"Okay," I whispered. I couldn't find my voice.

"Do you have any plastic grocery bags?"

"Yes, ma'am."

"Go get one and head to the bathroom."

I did as I was told. I had a plastic bag in the kitchenette area. I grabbed one and went to the bathroom. It still hadn't occurred to me to put on any clothes. I was still wrapped in a bath towel.

"I'm in the bathroom."

"Okay, good. Now I need you to scoop up the placenta and the baby into the plastic bag. Are you doing it?"

"Yes, ma'am," I lied. I heard her directions, but I couldn't muster up the courage to pick up my baby or the placenta. I walked over to the tub and stared at what used to be life. I couldn't touch her yet.

"Now tie the bag up. I want you to come home to see your doctor here, and I need you to bring the baby and the placenta with you. Do you understand?" Mama was calm. Her voice was like medicine for my hurting heart. "I need you to be strong, Robin. You can do this. Do you understand?"

"Yes, ma'am," I sobbed into the phone. I sat on the floor in a corner in the bathroom. I couldn't believe what was happening to me.

"Go ahead and get dressed, sweetheart. Get here as soon as you can so you can see the doctor today. It's important to get here today. You can drive, right?"

"Yes, ma'am." *It's not like I have a choice.*

"I love you. Call me when you are on your way. Are you okay?"

"Yes, ma'am," I lied.

When we ended the call, I sat there on the floor, still crying. I started pulling at my hair and covering my face almost simultaneously. I was literally about to lose it. I could feel it. To keep from losing my mind, I started whispering, "Jesus, Jesus, Jesus," over and over. I rocked back and forth, wailing, "Jesus, Jesus, Jesus," like a mantra until I felt a sense of peace. I don't know how long I sat there. Finally, I stopped rocking and looked at the tub. I must have looked like a mad woman. I had to scoop up the baby and placenta as my mom instructed. Even if I wanted to, I couldn't leave all of that in the bathroom for my roommates to find. I was traumatized.

I crawled over to the tub and looked inside. Mama told me I needed to be strong. *Lord, help me!* I hesitantly reached inside the tub to pick up the baby. She was about the size of a lemon. Her eyes had started developing as well as her nose and lips. She had two arms and two little hands developing. She had only one leg and a tiny foot. A small stub was where her right leg would have grown from. She felt rubbery and was pinkish opalescent in color. I held her in my palm and gently rubbed her stomach with my index finger. I knelt, pondering what her life would have been like and whether or not she was a girl. I felt like the baby was a girl. I didn't want to put her in the plastic bag like a piece of trash because she wasn't. She was a sweet little person who was no longer alive. Before I put her in the plastic bag, I whispered to her, "I love you, baby. I'll see you on the other side."

As I placed her in the bag, more tears escaped. I didn't try to control them. They demanded to fall, so I let them. I scooped up the placenta through teary, cloudy eyes. To soothe my bleeding heart, I again whispered, "Jesus, Jesus, Jesus," over and over.

After I tied the bag up, I began cleaning up the mess in the bathroom. I cleaned the tub, sink, and floor. I used a bleach cleaner I had specifically for cleaning the bathroom. After I finished cleaning, I got back in the shower to clean myself up. By the time I finished all of that, I was numb. I tried calling Kent several times to tell him what had happened, but he didn't answer the phone. I finally sent him a text, giving him details on what transpired. I said I was headed home to see my doctor.

His response was simple. It was something like, "I'm sorry you had to go through that. Be careful on the road." He was a jerk. He had been a jerk throughout the entire ordeal. I don't even know why I expected his response to be any different.

I got dressed in some sweatpants and a t-shirt. Before I walked out of the door, I grabbed another plastic bag to double bag my precious package just in case there was any leakage. I placed her in my purse and walked out of the door. I sent Cedric a text, saying I wasn't going to make it to class that day and asked him to take good notes. I didn't tell anyone else what was happening with me. I was ashamed. I had been foolish, and now I was paying the price for my foolishness. I deserved every ounce of pain that came my way because I didn't take heed to the warnings. I ignored every red flag and threw caution to the wind for the sake of "kickin' it" with a friend. *But God.*

    I drove home, listening to India Arie. She was my go-to artist when I was feeling down. Her voice is beautiful and soothing, calming to my spirit. I called my mom and said I was on the road. She instructed me to go straight to the women's clinic in Starkville. She had already called and made my appointment. Mom was amazing that day, just as amazing as she still is today. I don't think I would have made it through the morning without her. It took me about two-and-a-half hours to get to Starkville. When I arrived at the clinic, dread came over me. I didn't want to go in. It was like I was fifteen all over again, walking inside, filled with shame and regret. I did what my mama taught me to do, suck it up and go on. I got out of my Mountaineer and walked in. I signed in at the front desk and took a seat. I looked around the room and saw pregnant moms with wedding rings on, reading magazines, smiling, laughing, and talking. *Shame on me for getting myself caught up like this again.*

    As I was being called back, I caught a glimpse of a pregnant girl walking through the door. She was around fifteen or sixteen years old. I saw myself in her. I wondered if she was feeling the same shame I had felt at that age. I wondered if somebody told her she had messed up her life. I wondered how she was doing emotionally. I couldn't help but wonder if she was still in school with the determination to prove to everyone who counted her out already that she would not only survive it but thrive as well. Seeing her caused something inside me to leap. That was the first time I ever felt the urge to help someone who was going through what I had already experienced. I wanted to talk to her, but I didn't. I wanted to encourage her, but I couldn't. I was fighting my own battle. I was having a hard-enough time trying to encourage myself. I couldn't help her. I could barely help me. How could I help someone else feel whole when I wasn't? The perception I had of myself was skewed, especially in the situation I was currently in.

When I left the triage area, I was put in a room to wait for the doctor. The doctor I usually saw wasn't available that day, so I saw another one. I'll call him Dr. Lieberman. Dr. Lieberman was great at his job, but he wasn't personable. His bedside manner needed some work. I knew this because, during my last trimester with Ariel, I had to see each doctor before delivery just in case my doctor wasn't available. Dr. Lieberman walked into the room with my chart in his hands. He asked me to give him details about my pregnancy. I explained everything that had transpired over the last twenty-four hours with teary eyes and a trembling voice. He asked me to give him the plastic bag. He took it from my trembling hands and walked over to the counter. With his back to me, he put on a pair of gloves and opened it. I heard the plastic moving, but he was blocking my view of his hands.

He closed the bag and put it in the trash. I maintained my composure, but I wanted to yell at him for throwing my baby away—in front of me. *Damn, he could have waited until I left the room or something.* I lowered my head at what I'd just witnessed; more tears began falling. He turned to me holding a small clear

Resilient

plastic cup in his hand and asked, "When was your last meal?" I looked to see what was in the cup. There was a sample of my placenta in there. *So that's what he was doing.*

"I had a snack around two this morning."

"No more food or drink for the rest of the day. You're going to have a D&C today to get the remaining tissue out. I'll send the orders over to the hospital," he stated matter-of-factly. "Wait here for a moment."

With that, Dr. Lieberman turned on his heels and left the room. His nurse came in a few minutes later holding some papers. She handed them to me and said to take them to the hospital. I left the clinic and went to the hospital. Mom was there at work. I went to the emergency department and told her what the doctor said. At the time, I didn't know what a D&C was. She explained to me what was going to happen. D&C means dilation and curettage. It's a procedure the doctor performs to clear the uterine lining after a miscarriage. I'd never had surgery before. I was terrified of being put to sleep. What if I didn't wake back up? My mom did her best to calm my fears. She gave me one of those hugs that only your mama can give when you feel like crap. *This lady is amazing.*

Later that day, it was time for my surgery. Mom walked with me to get prepped for surgery. She stayed with me until it was time for the surgery team to roll me back to the operating room. She said everything was going to be all right, just like she always did. I had a sweet blonde haired, petite nurse named Anna. When I got into the operating room (OR), I was still awake. I started to cry, silent tears, of course. Anna noticed the tears and held my hand. She said, "It's going to be okay, sunshine." I couldn't see to my left or my right because I was lying flat on my back and couldn't move. She held her head over mine and looked into my eyes. She serenely said, "Just relax. Start counting backward from ten."

I started counting. Before I could get to seven, I was out like a light.

I was awakened in the OR by Anna saying, "Wake up, sunshine!" I heard her before I opened my eyes. I opened my eyes to a bright light, beaming down on me. "There you go, wake up!" she said.

I was parched. My throat was dry. Anna said I was about to go to recovery. I wanted to speak, but my throat was too dry. I was wheeled to recovery; my mom was right there, waiting for me. I was glad to see her.

After I was settled in, Mama got me some ice water. I took a few sips. It was like heaven! I don't think I had ever been so thirsty in my life. After being in recovery for a while, I had to use the restroom. That was a good thing because I wasn't going to be discharged to go home until I went. When I came out of the restroom, I heard a familiar voice say, "You left your gown open." I turned around to make sure my mind wasn't playing tricks on me.

It was Brandon! *What the hell?*

"What are you doing here?" I asked in utter shock.

"Your mom called my mom, so here I am. I came to check on you," he said with a sly smile.

"I'm doing all right," I said as I walked back to my bed. I looked at my mom with the "why did you call his mama" face.

"Hey, Brandon, how are you doing?" my mom asked.

"I'm doing good. How about you?"

"I'm fine. Thanks for coming by to check on my baby."

"No problem," he said while looking at me.

He didn't stay long. We made small talk about random stuff. I don't remember what we talked about. He stayed no more than fifteen to twenty minutes. When he left, I asked my mom why she called his mama. She said she was worried about me, and we needed all the prayers we could get. I couldn't argue there. I did need prayers, a lot of them. I was still upset about losing the baby. I was even more upset about the way Kent had treated me. I didn't know what to do with my emotions.

One thing was for certain, I didn't want to feel anything. I wanted to be numb. I was discharged from the hospital after the doctor came to examine me. He ordered some antibiotics and pain medication to be taken over the next few days.

I remained at home through the weekend. I'm not sure if my mom told my dad what I'd just gone through or not. He didn't bring it up, and neither did I. I spent the majority of my time with Ariel, watching television and going over her homework. I had material from school to study, but I didn't bother to pick it up. I was still trying to get my mind right to face each day. I had to get myself together before heading back to school.

My mom kept quiet and didn't bother me the entire weekend. I think she knew I just wanted to be left alone. However, before I left Sunday evening, Mom said she wanted to talk. She said some things I'll never forget. "That boy is not even worthy of speaking your name. He's a coward. He doesn't deserve you, and you should never speak to him again."

As I drove back to Memphis, I replayed what my mama said over and over in my head. She was right. The lies he'd told and the way he had treated me was beyond forgivable. Somewhere, way down on the inside of me, I knew I deserved better. I wanted better for myself, yet better was out of my reach. I couldn't touch it even if I wanted to. Maybe I didn't deserve it because I'd already made so many mistakes in my little twenty-three-and-a-half years of life. I decided on my way back that I was going to be by myself. If I chose to deal with another man, it was going to be on my terms and my terms alone. My heart was hardening, and the walls were up. They were up to protect me, and I'll be damned if I let another man come into my life to hurt me like that.

Resilient

February 11, 2006

Dear God,

It's me Robin. I've gotten myself into a world of trouble again. I should have listened when You told me to stop talking to Kent. It's because of my disobedience that I'm back in the same place again. I've been hurt, let down, and mistreated. It's like nobody cares about me or what I feel. Why do men treat me this way? Why do they consistently take advantage of my love? I have hurt on top of hurt. My daddy hurt me. Austin hurt me. Brandon hurt me. Now, Kent has hurt me. I guess I just can't get away from it. When will You send me someone to love me for who I am? When will You send me someone who will be there for me no matter what? Where is the man that will take care of my heart and not just throw it away? I'm tired, so very tired of being treated like I'm trash. I am a good person, but maybe, just maybe, I don't deserve to have the kind of love I desire. I've made terrible mistakes. I can't even look at myself in the mirror. I don't like what I see.

To make matters worse, I'm afraid that Ariel is going to hate me as she grows older. I'm hoping that she understands I left to go to school to make life better for her. She looks so sad every time I have to leave home to come back to Memphis. I want her to come live with me. I want her to know that I'm still here for her. The more I think about it, the more I just want it to be the two of us. No man in our lives at all. All men do is lie and cheat. Neither of us need that kind of drama. Besides, we can be like the Gilmore Girls on TV.

Lord, I know it's been a while since I've written, but I just want to say that I'm sorry. I had another slip-up in judgement, but of course, You knew that already. You knew even before I did. I don't think I ever want to speak to Kent again. Like Mama said, he's not worthy of speaking my name. It's funny how Mama can see he's not worthy of me, but I can't see how worthy I am. I don't feel worthy. I don't feel loved. I don't even feel forgiven half of the time. I should take this time to focus on other things like school. I should focus on what I want. I should focus on me. I'm tired of crying over these niggas. I'm tired of being disappointed. I'm done with love and trying to find it. I don't want it anymore. If this is what love is, they can have it.

XOXO

23

One Friday, I decided not to go home. I wanted to stay in Memphis to avoid seeing my family that weekend. I remember telling my mom that I had to study for a test. The following Saturday morning, I went to Tom Lee Park to see the Mississippi River. It was cold; the air was crisp outside. I took my journal with me just in case I felt like writing. I wrote in my journal that day as I sat on a bench crying my eyes out. I stared out into that water and thought about how peaceful it looked, but everyone knows the Mississippi River is a force to be reckoned with once you get in. I was like that river.

To look at me, one would think I had it all together, that my life was great, that I didn't have a care in the world. But to look into my soul, one would see the hurt, anger, bitterness, resentment, and shame dwelling there. I didn't let people get too close to me for this reason. There was no way they would be able to handle the demons

I fought within. That's why my circle was small. April was my circle, and even she didn't know the full depth of my depravity. After I finished pouring what was left of my heart out into my journal in tears and anguish, I made it my business to never cry like that again. And I didn't, not until 2018, but that's another story.

I finished the rest of the spring 2006 semester with grace. I buried all of my emotions so I wouldn't feel anything. If a tear tried to fall, I immediately reeled it in. If my mind tried to go into deep thought about anything concerning my life, I immediately changed my train of thought to focus on something else. I had emotionally shut down. I didn't pray about it. I didn't pray much about anything pertaining to my heart. I focused my prayers solely on Ariel and getting done with school so that I could take care of her.

I studied and hung out with Cedric and Sam a lot. Those two were there for me; they made my social life bearable in pharmacy school. I didn't hang out or talk to a lot of females in my class. I studied here and there with a couple of girls, but I didn't vibe with anyone there. If it weren't for Cedric and Sam, I probably would have been a recluse. I sat next to Cedric in every class. His friendship was comforting to me. He made me laugh all the time. During that time, our friendship was strictly platonic. My head and heart weren't ready for anything serious; I had no desire to love or be in love again. I was done with love and anything pertaining to it.

When I saw Kent, I kept things polite and casual. However, I always imagined punching his ass in the face. I needed God's help. I needed emotional healing like never before. So, to try to get my spiritual self together, I attended "The Threshing Floor" conference in Atlanta, GA, with April. We had just been through a lot. Her dad had passed away; her life wasn't going the way she thought it should. I'd just lost a baby, and I had feelings I did not want to deal with. We both wanted a refreshing. We both needed a refreshing.

    I was weighed down. I could feel God nudging at me to spend time with Him like I did when I was first saved, but my shame kept me from reaching out to Him. The enemy has a way of beating us up about our past mistakes. Satan was wearing me out. My shame and regret kept me from running to the Father I knew could help me. I wanted to be better, but I had been in a cycle of disobedience and feeling guilty from my past sins. I was haunted and taunted daily in my own prison. I had forgiven myself before I made another stupid mistake but all of that self-forgiveness went out the window. The Threshing Floor conference was amazing. I left there feeling refreshed and stronger. I felt like I could take on the world. I heard messages from Bishop Tudor Bismark, Bishop T.D. Jakes, Dr. Cindy Trimm, and Darlene Bishop, to name a few. The Word was so good that weekend, I had given Satan a run for his money. Or so I thought.

    Shortly after returning from the conference, I decided to make a change. I wanted out of living on campus. I told my parents I was going to find an apartment off-campus. Ultimately, I decided on moving back to the Mississippi side of the state line and moved into my apartment over the summer. Ariel and one of her friends came to stay with me for a few days. It was good to be back in my own space. Having roommates wasn't too bad, but I'd always been a private person. I didn't like people in my space. Let's just call it a character flaw. Since I had an apartment, I wanted Ariel to come live with me. But again, I let her stay with my parents because they thought it was best for us.

    I didn't see Cedric much over the summer of 2006, but I did

talk to him often. I missed him a little bit, and it was buggin' me. One day, he did come over to my apartment to keep me company while I put some bookshelves together. We laughed, talked, and had a great time together. I kept looking at him, thinking about what it would be like if we were a couple. But I pushed those thoughts aside as quickly as they came. Besides, he was seeing someone and seemed happy. On top of that, I wasn't ready to be in a serious relationship anyway.

By the time August rolled around, I was all settled in and ready to take on a new semester of school. I was focused and excited. Also, by August (actually before August), I had started back communicating with Kent. We didn't talk every day or hang out a lot like we had in the past, but I fell right back into the same cycle of stupidity all because he was someone I was "comfortable" with. When I told April I had started back communicating with him, she said, "Why in the hell are you talking to him, Robin? That's dumb! I can't believe you are giving him the time of day."

"It'll just be for sex. I don't want to add a new guy to my repertoire of guys I've slept with. I'm not falling in love or anything. It'll just be sex, and it'll only be when I want to. I know what I'm doing."

"That makes no sense, Robin! Sex is not that good."

"I know, but what can I say? That's the only reason I'm dealing with this dude."

"Okay, well, whatever."

Then I changed the subject to talk about medical school. April had been accepted into medical school in Illinois. It was an exciting time for her. I was happy for her. Things were looking up for the both of us. My life was going as usual until April called me

Resilient

in October saying she was pregnant. I had no words! She had just started medical school. The timing was the absolute worst. I tried to comfort her with words of encouragement by telling her it would be all right, but nothing I said brought her solace. All I could do was pray for her. She didn't see how she would be able to stay in school or be able to care for her unborn child. I talked to her every single day to make sure she was all right. It was an extremely tough time for her. I tried every day to be a ray of sunshine for her. I wanted her and the baby to be okay. She was my best friend. If something wasn't right with her, something wasn't right with me and vice versa. I needed her to be okay so that I would be okay. Only true BFFs will understand what I'm saying here. If you don't get it, that's fine.

By the end of November, things had settled a little bit with April. It was time for Thanksgiving. I cooked dinner at my apartment for Cedric, Sam, and Tracy. We had greens, chicken & dressing, ham, and macaroni and cheese (one of Cedric's favorites). We had our dinner before I left to go home to have Thanksgiving dinner with my family. Dinner was great! Kent called and asked what I was doing. I told him about my dinner, so he wanted to come over and get a plate. I didn't want him there, but I didn't want to possibly hurt his feelings by telling him he couldn't come.

Once again, I had put someone else's feelings before my own. I fixed a plate for him and set it to the side. Anyway, when he got there, the energy in the room shifted. Cedric and Sam weren't too thrilled about him being there, especially after what had previously happened. Their faces said it all. They knew Kent was no good for me and couldn't understand why I was associating myself with him. God, I should have listened to my friends.

While the guys remained inside, Tracy and I went out on the balcony. Tracy expressed her interest in Cedric to me.

"He's cute," she said. "Does he have a girlfriend?"

"Yes, he does. But, even if he didn't, you can't talk to him."

"Why not?"

"Because I like him … a lot."

"Well, why do you have this other nigga up in here eating then?"

"I don't know! He was hungry, so I told him he could come to get a plate," I replied shame-faced.

"You need to drop this dude, girl, and tell Cedric how you feel before somebody else ends up with him!"

She was right. I should have told Cedric, but I didn't think I was good enough for him. To date, I had not made the best decisions. I felt like he needed to be with someone who didn't have so much baggage. I wasn't about to risk getting my feelings hurt. Besides, I didn't want to be in love anyway, and Cedric deserved someone who could love him the way he deserved to be loved. He was a good guy. I wasn't about to mess over him. When everybody left, Kent hung around. He tried to get some and spend the night, but I told him I wasn't in the mood. I sent him home.

I thought a lot about what my mom, April, Tracy, Cedric, and Sam had said about my dealings with Kent. They were right. Why was I still on this path with him that ultimately would lead to nowhere? I was over it. It was time to put an end to it. It was about time to see myself the way God saw me. Whole. Healed. And Complete. I was going to go into 2007 without Kent in my life and looking forward to it. And 2007 would be a new start. So, I opted for what I called "goodbye sex."

Resilient

God was telling me no. But once again, I was hard-headed. After all, it was just one last time. I had timed it perfectly. My cycle had just ended a few days before, so I wasn't ovulating. I didn't want to make the mistake of getting pregnant again, and since I wasn't ovulating, it would be near impossible. So, I had sex with him. It wasn't even good. *What a waste!*

I wasn't into it, anyway; that's probably why I didn't enjoy myself. *Oh, well.*

The next day, I thought about going to buy a Plan B, an emergency contraceptive to prevent pregnancy. But, since I was sure I wasn't ovulating, I didn't worry about it. I didn't give it a second thought. I didn't talk to Kent as promised anymore after that night. I went home for the last couple of weeks of the year and enjoyed time with my family. I told April about my last little tryst with Kent and that I was glad to be done with him. I had no feelings for him, no emotion whatsoever, and I was glad to be moving on.

I was ready to enjoy my singleness and not be depressed about it. I was going to walk it out alone, graduate from pharmacy school, buy my little C-Class Mercedes Benz, and enjoy my life with my daughter. That was my plan. Enjoying life without a companion and love were the lies I had to feed myself to accept that maybe I would never be married. Maybe I would never know what it was like to be loved by someone and cared for despite all of my flaws or to have someone accept my daughter and love her as his own. I was accepting the fact it might just be Ariel, me, and no one else. Kent had further proven a theory I had come up with a long time ago, that true love does not exist. My plans to live in solitude were in full effect now.

Oh, but God undoubtedly has a way of throwing monkey

wrenches in my plans. When January came around and my period didn't flow on the day it was supposed to, I took a pregnancy test.

I was pregnant! I laughed and asked, "Really, Lord? Really? You have got to be kidding me! I wasn't even ovulating!" I couldn't believe this was happening to me again. I had planned it out for goodness sake. I was pissed. I could have kicked myself for not going with my first thought and taking Plan B. I had to take a seat to process what I saw on the EPT stick. I had to think and get myself together because now my life was about to get that much harder as if it wasn't hard enough already. Now I was going to be a single mother of two with two "baby daddies."; a label I didn't want to wear. Women get frowned upon all of the time for having more than one father for their children. Now, I was going to be one of those women.

I kept the news to myself for a few days until I could sort out my feelings. I called and told my mom first and then April. I cried as I talked to April because I did not want to be pregnant. I was now going through the same thing I was trying to comfort her through a few months ago. It was now her turn to comfort me. We cried about our problems. We were pitiful.

Mama's response was comical. She asked, "Is it for that beady-eyed boy?" I laughed and said it was. "What are you going to do, honey?" I said I was going to keep the baby and finish school. Then Mama said that she and Daddy would help out any way they could.

Next, I had to seek out a doctor. I had insurance with the school, but I didn't think it would cover maternity care. I applied for Mississippi Medicaid and was approved within a month. Before I got approval, I went to see a doctor in Olive Branch. His staff was nasty. I said I'd just found out I was pregnant and had applied for Medicaid but didn't have my card yet. The receptionist charged me $500 to be seen that day. I should have walked out of the door, but I paid it because I wanted to be examined as soon as possible. The doctor's attitude wasn't much better than that of the receptionist. I left the office with a prescription for prenatal vitamins.

About a week later, I had some vaginal bleeding and called the office. The receptionist wouldn't give me an appointment to come in. I called during office hours, so why couldn't I get an appointment? She was being a real you-know-what. After going back and forth with her for a minute or two, I told her to have a good day and hung up the phone. She was still talking, but I didn't care to hear what she was saying.

I went to the emergency room, signed in, and told the receptionist I was pregnant and spotting. You would think that I would have been called right back after a few minutes; but no, I sat there for over an hour, waiting. I was the only person waiting, other than another lady groaning in pain. I called my mom to tell her what was going on. Yes, I called my mom for just about everything. Anyway, she wanted to know which hospital I was at. I told her; she said she would call me back. I don't know who my mama talked to or what she said, but maybe five minutes later, a petite older woman opened one of the doors that led to rooms and walked over to me. She said she was sorry I had to wait for so long, but someone would be calling me back shortly. I said, "Thank you," and she walked away.

Mom called me back like clockwork and asked if anyone had come to speak with me. Mama started going off about how I was being mistreated and everything. She had spoken to the house supervisor; I'm pretty sure she let her have it. Mama said there was no way I should have been sitting there that long being pregnant and bleeding. If I didn't get called back within fifteen minutes, I was to call her back and let her know. As soon as we ended the call, I was called back to triage. Once again, my mother had amazed me.

It turned out that my baby was fine. I was given instructions to follow-up with my healthcare provider within the next week. Because there was no way in hell that I was going back to the doctor I had just seen, I found a new doctor. Dr. Hamner was a tall older, African American gentleman who wore glasses. He was great; his staff was great. I had to wait a long while to see him during my first visit, but he was worth the wait. He was reassuring with excellent bedside manner; we even had a full conversation. By the end of my first visit, he was calling me kiddo. His first question to me was, "How are you feeling today?"

"I'm doing good."

He started going over my medical history again, as I had already given it to the nurse.

"How many pregnancies?"

"Three"

"Live births?"

"One birth, one abortion, one miscarriage."

"Age at first pregnancy?"

"Fifteen."

He wasn't trying to, but I felt like I was being scrutinized because I still held on to the shame from my past. After he asked my family's medical history, he inquired about my last period. When I told him, he pulled out his pregnancy wheel to give me the date of conception and my approximate due date.

"Looks like you got pregnant on December 31, and your due date will be around September 25 or so."

"I didn't have sex on December 31," I said matter-of-factly.

"Sometimes you might ovulate a day or two early or late, that's been known to happen."

"I didn't have sex anywhere near that date, not before or after. I had sex a little over a week before the thirty-first."

"Okay, well you are indeed pregnant regardless of the date you had sex, kiddo."

I said okay, but all I could think was, *How does sperm live nine to ten days? Where does this happen at?* I was no expert, but I was sure that I'd read somewhere that sperm doesn't live that long. I just had to accept it. God undeniably had His hand in that one. When I told my mom, she laughed and said, "I guess that baby is meant to be here."

I had a follow-up appointment for three weeks out and another prescription for prenatal vitamins with iron.

Resilient through Fear…

Robin Terry

24

It was time to tell the next person closest to me about my pregnancy. I waited until we got to class and sat down to get settled in for our lecture. I always sat to the right of Cedric, so when I leaned in close to him, it wasn't a surprise. As he was taking his notebook out of his backpack, I whispered in his ear, "I'm pregnant." I had been afraid to tell him, of all people, because I didn't know what his reaction would be. I did, however, know, without a doubt, he would be disappointed in me. I had told him I was done with Kent, but I never mentioned how I slept with him from time to time.

"What? Girl, what are you doing?" he half-whispered, frowning, shaking his head.

"It was an accident." I felt the shame creeping back upon me. It was time for class to start. I didn't know what he was thinking, but he was my friend. I didn't need his approval, but I wanted it. I wanted him to tell me everything would work out.

During class, we started writing notes back and forth. I explained the whole "not having sex during ovulation thing." What could I say? I was thrown for a loop as well. Before the end of the lecture, he wrote that everything would work out.

I got around to telling Sam later. I'm sure the guys discussed it between themselves. Whatever they said to each other, I'll never know. Kent was the last in my circle to be informed about my pregnancy. I went to his apartment on campus to speak with him face to face. I don't even remember sitting down. I remember remaining close to the doorway. When I told him, his response was nonchalant. But then he asked, "Did you do this on purpose?"

"I'm in pharmacy school, and I already have a child. Why would I do this on purpose?" I asked angrily. "You're not the cream of the crop. I'm not trying to trap you; I don't want a damn thing from you. This baby is mine and mine alone. You can go on and live your life however you want to live it! I'm not asking you for a damn thing. This baby and I will be just fine. Don't get it twisted!" I was fuming. "My parents have enough money to help me take care of this baby until I graduate from school. Whatever I ain't got, they got, and they won't let us go without anything."

He was looking at me like he couldn't believe what he was hearing. I continued, "Better yet, what I look like deliberately messing up my own life trying to trap you? I came to pharmacy school to get my life, not ruin it. So, don't do that! Don't nobody want you that bad!" I said smirking.

With my last remark, I left. For him to think I would do something like that on purpose was upsetting. I'm not a gold digger. I've always been about my business, especially since I had a daughter depending on me to make it.

Resilient

After I told him about my pregnancy, I didn't spend any more time with Kent. I didn't go out with him. I had neither food nor drink in his presence. I'd barely spoken to Kent since informing him that I was pregnant. Considering I felt like he put something in my drink to cause me to miscarry before, I didn't want to risk something similar happening again. Even after he called to apologize, I kept my distance.

Meanwhile, I was spending the majority of my free time with Cedric and sometimes Sam. Cedric regularly checked in on me. He wanted to make sure I was doing well. He made sure I was cared for and listened to me go on and on about whatever I was feeling. He was there. He was present. He steadied me. The more time I spent with him, the more he doted on me, and the more the steel bars around my heart started to come down. While I was still guarded with everyone else, I became less guarded with him. I didn't know if Cedric had feelings for me or not, but his actions certainly showed he did.

One night that I'll never forget, he came to my rescue. First, let me say that I am afraid of spiders, big or small, brown or black, real or fake, it doesn't matter. I am afraid of spiders. I always keep bug spray handy. Well, I got up one night to leave my bedroom to get some water from the kitchen and saw this big ass brown spider on my floor, next to the return vent of the HVAC unit. I ran to get my bug spray. Before I could spray it good, it crawled into the vent. I was terrified! I was tired and couldn't go to sleep because I was thinking about the spider coming out of the vent over my bed to bite me. I'm sure it was my hormones overreacting, but I couldn't rest.

I called my mom in a crying frenzy. Yes, I was overly dramatic in a spider crisis. She said, "Baby, what do you want me to do? I'm two hours away?" She said it was probably dead anyway since I had sprayed it a little bit. Well, I still wasn't satisfied with her response. I thought about calling Kent.

Hell naw! I'm not calling him! I don't want him anywhere near me. I thought about calling Sam, but thought, *Nah, he won't come.* I stood there in the middle of my living room crying. Then I thought about Cedric. I called Cedric.

"Hello," he said in a low deep voice.

"There's a spider here. I tried to kill it, but it crawled under the vent thing. Now I can't go to sleep." I cried on the phone.

"Girl, what? You calling me about a spider? I'm already in the bed." He sounded a little aggravated.

"Yeah, I sprayed it. But I don't think I got it. Now I can't find it, and I can't go to sleep." I was still crying.

"Just try to go to sleep."

"I can't." I was still crying. Normally, I would not have behaved that way. But because of my pregnancy, it may have been my hormones.

"Okay, I'll be there in a little bit."

"Really?" My tears started drying up. "Okay."

I stood in my living room with all the lights on until he arrived about thirty minutes later. He came in and asked me to show him where the spider was. I pointed to the area. He got my bug spray and walked around my entire apartment, spraying the corners and baseboards. Then he said to pack up some clothes so that I could go to his apartment. I fell in love that night. I already had feelings for him. But that night, I completely let my guard down. I was like putty in his hands, and he didn't even know it.

As we drove back to his place, I thought, *Surely, he must*

have feelings for me because only love would make a man get out of his bed close to midnight and drive from East Memphis to Southaven to kill a spider. Only love would have a man tell me to pack a bag to spend the night at his place so that I could get some sleep.

I didn't tell him what I was feeling, nor did I ask him why he was so good to me. I didn't want to take the chance of ruining our friendship. Cedric lived in a two-bedroom, one-bathroom apartment. He had Bible verses that he'd written down or typed taped to the walls throughout the place. It always smelled great because Glade Plug-ins were always plugged into the outlets. He had nice furniture, and his place was always clean. When we got back to his apartment, he said I could sleep in his bed. He went into his guest bedroom to lay down, but he couldn't get comfortable. He came and got into bed with me. He didn't try anything; he was the perfect gentleman. He just lay there next to me, and that made me appreciate him all the more. I nestled into the comfort of his bed and drifted off to sleep.

By the time I started to show, some of my classmates had started asking if I was pregnant. It was like high school all over again. Because I had lived through it before, it didn't bother me much this time. Naturally, when people are nosey, they never go directly to the source. They always ask someone else. So, they asked the people closest to me, Cedric and Sam. Of course, my boys told me what was going on. They would say they were both the father. I laughed at their subtle ways of trying to protect me. It wasn't anybody's business who the father of my child was, especially since not a single one of them would be helping me care for my baby.

In March, we had a trip coming up for school. Two conferences were going on at the same time. Cedric went to the APhA-ASP (American Pharmacists Association-Academy of

Student Pharmacists) conference in Atlanta, and I went to the SNPhA (Student National Pharmaceutical Association) conference in Denver. It was going to be my first time away from him, and I was missing him already. Before it was time to leave school for the conference, I ran into him in the hallway of the General Education Building. I was walking with Juliette, a medical student and one of Cedric's friends from undergrad, to the computer lab. Cedric and I were seeing each other off. I went in for a hug before leaving, but he instead went in for a kiss. He kissed me on my lips, no tongue or anything, and held me closer than a friend should and squeezed me tightly. I melted in his arms and did not want him to let me go. When he finally released me, I blushed. I didn't know what to say. The kiss was unexpected, but I liked it; I wanted him to do it again. Then Cedric looked into my eyes and said, "Be careful and come back safely."

He told Juliette, "I'll see you later," and walked away.

Kent also went to the SNPhA conference. I can't remember if I knew beforehand that he was going or not, but I remember running into him at the opening reception. He walked up to me while I was talking to someone else and asked, "What are you drinking?"

"Water," I stated dryly.

"No cocktail tonight?"

"No, I'm drinking more water these days."

The girl I was talking to looked down at my protruding belly and eyed Kent but didn't say anything. Then she walked away, saying she would see me later. My belly wasn't huge. Because I had been pregnant three times before, I started showing pretty early since I was just out of my first trimester. I don't recall seeing much of Kent after the opening reception. I'm not sure if it was because I was avoiding him or not. I don't remember deliberately avoiding him. I just didn't see him. I honestly don't remember much about that trip other than eating some asparagus during dinner that made my stomach hurt. I spent a lot of my time missing Cedric, wondering what he was doing and thinking about that kiss. I talked to him a couple of times and couldn't wait to get back home to him. I didn't tell him about my growing feelings. I wasn't in the best situation. I was pregnant by another man; a man I couldn't stand to be around.

When we got back from our respective trips, we were together all of the time. We were together every single day. I told April how close we were getting. I wanted to be with him, but I was afraid he wouldn't want to be with me because I already had children by two different men. That's something I was ashamed of. My many issues still practically defined me, and I didn't feel worthy of having a man like him.

April said I was being absurd, and I deserved to have a good man who loved my children and me. I tried to let her words overshadow my negative thoughts, but it was hard to do. I had gotten accustomed to being treated like trash. It was hard to believe someone would want to treat me well.

Cedric, however, was consistently proving me to be wrong. He checked on me all of the time. He brought me food. He rubbed my back. If I said I needed something, he made sure I had it. It was crazy. He was different from every other man who had been in my life. He didn't drink too much. He didn't mistreat me. He didn't talk down to me. He really proved himself. The more he proved himself, the more I felt unworthy. I didn't know my worth back then. I had been badly scarred, and my perception was skewed; I couldn't see that he was the one who needed to prove he was worthy of me. I had plenty to bring to the table. I was smart. I was strong. I was beautiful. I loved the Lord. However, I felt like I wasn't worthy of being loved. That feeling of worthlessness started when I was fifteen. I was still holding on to it some ten years later.

Although I had forgiven my daddy for the way he treated me, the residue from the hurt was still there. Maybe that was why I'd chosen to remain in relationships that weren't good for me. I didn't expect any better because I hadn't been treated any better at the beginning of the hardship I had caused in my life. So, yes, I was afraid that like all the others, Cedric would see my worthlessness and start treating me as such.

After thinking about how my life was going, I'd made up my mind that once I had my baby, I was going to get my tubes tied and focus on raising my two children alone. After all, Ariel was getting older. I didn't want to risk bringing someone into our lives who would want my daughter more than he wanted me. There were stories all over the news about little girls being raped or molested by their mothers' boyfriends or husbands. It was freaking me out, especially being a single mom. *These days you don't know if a man wants you or if he wants your kid.* When I told Cedric, Sam, and Tracy my plan and the reason behind it one night over dinner, they all thought I was crazy. I just didn't trust anyone with us. I was sticking to my guns.

***

After some time and despite my fears, I went out on a limb and took April's advice to tell Cedric how I felt and to let him love me (if he really wanted to). I didn't tell him right away. I waited

Resilient

until after I gave him a rundown of my life's story.

I had driven over to his apartment to hang out. We spent more time talking than we did studying that day. After we had eaten, we sat around and talked some more. That's when the rundown of my life story began. I sat there with my rounded belly, telling how I'd gotten pregnant at fifteen and the struggles I had because of it. I told him about Trevor and everything that happened with Brandon. Of course, he already knew the story with Kent. I waited for his reaction from hearing all the drama associated with my life. All he said was something like, "That's all in the past. You're strong, and you're still making it. They didn't know how to treat you. They didn't know what they had."

I didn't know what to say to that. I stared at Cedric, trying to figure out if he could really love me. Would he know what he'd have if we wound up being together? He caught my gaze, but then I changed the subject. I slept at his apartment that night in his guest room. I didn't fall asleep right away this time. I was awake in bed, looking at the ceiling, trying to figure out what the hell I was doing.

Before the spring semester 2007 ended, I finally told Cedric what I was feeling. We were talking on the phone when I told him that I wanted to be with him. I said, "I love you and want us to be together."

He was already seeing someone else, so I asked him not to say anything. I just wanted him to think about it. I'm not sure how things were going with her. I didn't see him talking on the phone to her as much as he used to. He didn't even talk about her anymore; I didn't exactly know his relationship status. I didn't even want to know. We didn't talk about it again for a while. We did, however, start kissing more. He rubbed my swollen belly more, cuddled, and hugged me more. We did everything but have sex. We were together one afternoon. He looked at me and said, "This is me! I'm not muscular and built like what you're used to having. Are you sure this is what you want?"

Cedric had let his guard down as well as I had. I looked at him and said from the bottom of my heart, "I'm sure. I love every part of you. Your weight doesn't matter to me. I love you for who you are." We kissed but still did not have sex that day. We both wanted security and unconditional love. We were willing to give it, but we were afraid that one would somehow fail the other. Although he never told me his insecurities, I saw them.

Neither of us let our insecurities keep us away from each other. We still spent more and more time together. We talked about our childhoods, parents, friends, faith, and different things that had gone on in our lives before knowing each other. He had interesting stories just like I did. He was telling me all of his business, and I was telling him all of mine. We had a great connection with no judgment. I appreciated the fact that he didn't pass judgment on me as I had already judged myself ten times over.

Even though he still hadn't said it, he showed me that he loved me by doing things with me. For example, I loved going to Tom Lee Park to see the Mississippi River. Although he wasn't a fan of being outside, he went with me. He'd walk with me and hold my hand. He also bought me purses and shoes, and he took me to expensive dinners. I said I didn't need all of those things. I didn't! The gifts were nice, but I really just wanted unconditional and undying love. Don't get me wrong; I love receiving gifts. What girl doesn't? But we were in school with limited incomes. I didn't want him spending his money foolishly. Nevertheless, to him, it wasn't a big deal. He wanted me to have it, so he bought it.

***

Before it was time for Kent to graduate, he called me toward the end of May, saying he wanted to give me some notes I could use to study for school. I reluctantly agreed to let him bring them to my apartment. I was expecting to see Cedric that afternoon, and I didn't want any interference. I made sure I was appropriately dressed for his visit. I closed the door to my bedroom and remained in the living room. He came in carrying a bunch of papers and a large notebook filled with more papers. I offered him a seat on the couch.

As I was walking to sit down, I noticed him looking at my stomach. It had grown a lot since the last time I saw him. I hadn't seen him since the previous month after telling him I was having a boy. When I found out I was having a boy, I already knew I was naming him after my dad. When I told Kent that I was going to name my son Robert Caleb, he didn't like it. Of course, I didn't give a shit. This was *my* baby, and I was going to name *my* baby whatever I wanted to name *my* baby — end of story.

Anyway, I digressed. We spent maybe five minutes going through the notes. I was trying to hurry it up. I didn't want him there when Cedric got there. All of a sudden, Kent decided he wanted to make small talk. Then my phone rang with Cedric's ringtone. I didn't know if I should answer or not since Kent was there. I was more concerned about how Cedric would feel if he knew Kent was there. Would he get upset with me? *Forget it. Kent's not my man. I need to talk to Cedric.*

I answered the phone with my usual smile. "Hello."

"Hey, what you doin'?" Cedric asked.

"Oh, nothing. Kent is over here. He brought some notes I could use to study. What are you doing?" I cringed, hoping he wasn't about to go off on me. I didn't want any secrets between us. I was honest. I didn't want him to think I was doing something behind his back. Technically, Cedric and I weren't in a relationship, but I'd already said I loved him and wanted to be with him. I didn't want him thinking I was lying or playing games.

It took a moment, but he finally said, "I'm on the road, headed back up that way."

"Oh, I thought you would have been here by now." I was disappointed. "What time will you be here?"

"I just left, so it'll be a while. I'll call you when I make it."

"Okay, then," I said slowly. I couldn't gauge his mood. I didn't know what to think. So, I didn't press the issue. "I'll talk to you later."

"Bye."

"Bye."

When my call with Cedric ended, Kent was looking at me like he was trying to figure out who I was talking to. It wasn't his business. I didn't offer up that information.

"Are you hungry? Do you want to go get something to eat?" Kent asked as he stared into my eyes.

"No, I'm not hungry."

"Do you want to go to the movies or something?"

"No, nothing is playing that I want to see," I said. *I'm not going anywhere with you.*

"Okay, well, I guess I'll get going," he said as he stood up. I remained seated. I didn't want him thinking he could hug me or anything.

"Okay, well, thank you for the notes. I'll get good use out of them."

"All right, take care." He walked to the door, slowly opened it, and left. That was the last time I saw him from that day to this one. I spent the rest of the afternoon waiting for Cedric to call me back. When he finally did, all was well.

25

During the summer of 2007, I had to complete what was called an institutional rotation at one of the hospitals affiliated with UT College of Pharmacy before I could start my practical rotations later during my education. Overall, I enjoyed the experience. But there was one pharmacy technician, Dorinda, who made me feel bad about myself. She was an older lady, maybe in her late fifties or early sixties.

My stomach was large, as one would suspect for almost seven months of pregnancy. I already didn't like some of the looks I was getting because I didn't have a ring on my finger, she only made it worse.

One day, Dorinda asked me, "Is this your first baby?"

"No, ma'am. I have a daughter."

"Are you married?

"No, ma'am."

"Are you with your baby's father?"

"No, ma'am."

"Oh, so you was just being fast then, wasn't you?" She asked with a sneer.

"No, ma'am," I responded and walked away. There it was again, shame lifting its ugly head, and me being stereotyped. I could not get away from it, no matter how hard I tried. There was always going to be somebody to remind me that I wasn't worthy. I remember telling Cedric about what she said, and he said, "Don't worry about it, that's just the way old people think."

Yeah, well, it still didn't make me feel any better.

Before it was time for the fall semester to start in August, I had gone to my hometown for a few weeks. Before I left, Cedric and I had a serious conversation about our relationship.

"Can't we just be friends and raise the baby together?" he asked.

"What do you mean?"

"I can help you take care of Caleb and everything. We can still be friends without us being together. I can be a father figure for him. I can take him to get his hair cut, buy him clothes, and spend time with him. I can do everything a father does."

"Without us being together?" I asked, confused.

"Yes."

"Well, what happens when you meet someone else and get married? You'll just disappear?" I asked, my heart was breaking.

"No, I wouldn't disappear. I would tell her that I'm helping you take care of your son."

"So, I'm supposed to watch the man I love marry someone else and hope that he will stick around and help me raise my son?"

I asked, but it wasn't actually a question.

"We would still be friends, though."

I didn't like what I was hearing, but I had to accept it. It sounded like Cedric was saying he didn't want to be in a relationship with me. He just wanted to be friends. I couldn't blame him, especially since I came as a package deal.

"I love you, Cedric, and I want us to be together. If we are not going to be together, there is no point in you helping me raise my children. It just wouldn't work. We can be regular friends, and I'll raise my children on my own. We will be fine." I said, holding back my tears.

When we ended the call, I cried and then did what I knew how to do best. I sucked it up and moved forward. I didn't talk to him much after that conversation. We needed the time apart.

I spent time with Ariel and the rest of my family for the remainder of the summer. Ariel was excited about having a baby brother. I was getting more excited, as well. I was fearful about my future; however, my mom assured me everything was going to be all right. I remember having a terrible dream that Caleb was going to die. In the dream, something was coming after me while I was still pregnant. It was trying to take my baby away from me, but then I saw an angel. He said his name was Michael. He said not to worry because he was protecting my baby and me. I awakened from the dream, feeling troubled by it but relieved an angel was there. When I told my mom about it, she got some oil, prayed over me, and said, "Everything is fine. The angel in the dream said so."

I went to church on Sunday, not in the best mood, but I enjoyed the service. After church, we went to Dionne's apartment for dinner. Mama was hanging around to go back to the six o'clock service that evening. She wanted me to go, but I wasn't in the mood. I told her I was not going. Right before it was time to leave, LaChrisa, a friend of ours from church, asked me once again to go. I was like, "Yeah, yeah. I'll go."

The second service was better than the first one. Elder Henderson called me to the front while he was still preaching. At first, I didn't know he was talking to me. He called me again, and I started looking around thinking, *Who is he talking to?* I'd never been picked out of a crowd; it was all new to me. Someone tapped me on my shoulder and said, "He's talking to you."

I got up and walked to the front, trembling. I had no idea what he was going to say to me. I stood at the altar alone while he was still preaching. *Maybe he wasn't talking to me. Let me go sit down.*

As I turned to walk back to my seat, he said, "Don't you go anywhere. I have a word for you. Margaret, Dionne, prayer warriors, come here."

Before I knew it, my mom, my sister, LaChrisa, and a couple of other women were around me. I wanted to hide. I do not like being the center of attention. I couldn't run from this, from whatever he was about to say. Elder Henderson walked up to me and said, "Lift your hands."

I did as instructed. He began prophesying to me, and I began to cry. I don't remember everything he said, but I remember him saying, "You are saved, and your baby is saved, even before he gets here. God has a plan for you and that baby. Don't you worry." That's how I knew God had heard me. Those words were comforting to my soul. I felt like shouting all over the altar; I couldn't because my baby was heavy. I was not trying to hurt him or myself. I left the church that night feeling refreshed and renewed. I had hope and renewed faith that all would be well with my children and me, even if I had to raise them alone.

I'd read a Scripture many times that said, "When my father and my mother forsake me, Then the LORD will take care of me (Psalms 27:10 NKJV)." My mother and father were in my life, but my children didn't have a father. What that promise said to me is that even though the fathers of my children had chosen not to be present, my children would not go without. God would step in to meet every need. All I had to do was continue to trust Him, and that is what I did.

***

Before it was time for me to head back to school in August, my mom and Dionne surprised me with a baby shower at Dionne's apartment. I thought we were all just getting together for a cookout with our friends from church. It was so sweet; it made me cry. Right after my surprise was out of the bag, we heard a knock at the door. My sister opened the door, and I got another surprise. Cedric walked in, carrying a large box with a car seat and stroller combo inside. I was speechless. I couldn't stop smiling.

After the conversation we had, I thought I wasn't going to see him again until class started. He set the box down, walked toward me, gave me a kiss, a hug, and then sat down next to me. All of the ladies were trying to figure out if he was my baby's father. One of them finally asked, "Is that your baby daddy?"

I replied, "No," and moved on to opening the gifts. We played games, ate cake, laughed, loved, and had a barrel of fun.

Before Cedric left, he pulled a few hundred dollars out of his pocket and gave it to me. He took the huge box back out with him. I wouldn't have enough room in my SUV for it along with all of the other stuff I'd gotten. I was so happy to see Cedric; I didn't know what to think. I didn't ask him any questions, though. It wasn't the right time. I just enjoyed the moment. I figured I would have a talk with him about it later.

When I made it back to my apartment, I sent a text to let Cedric know I had arrived safely. He was at work. He called me when he got off and said he would be coming over. It was after eight o'clock; I was already in bed when he showed up. He came in, carrying his bag, and stated, "I'm going to take a shower."

I planned to talk to him when he got out of the shower, but I hadn't figured out how to express my concerns to him. He kissed my lips and then my neck. To sum it up, he made love to me that night. It was wonderful. Once I came down from my lovemaking high, I started to feel an emptiness inside. I lay there thinking while he was sound asleep. I thought about how he said he couldn't be in a relationship with me, yet he'd just made love to me. I had to tell him that what had just happened, wasn't going to happen again. It would be like history repeating itself in my life if I remained on this path with him. Sex with no relationship or commitment; I didn't want that anymore. Not this time around.

I planned to talk to him the next day about it. Before I could get the words out, he said, "I ended things with Danita because I'm in love with you. I made love to you. We're together."

Well, there was no need for the conversation I was ready to have. I said, "Okay," with a smile; I couldn't have been happier.

26

On September 13, I woke up early in the morning with labor pain. I had started feeling slight back pain and mild cramping before going to bed. I assumed it was Braxton Hicks contractions because I wasn't due for another week or so. I remember telling Cedric I didn't want to have the baby on September 13. That date was such a sad date on the calendar for me. That was the date I'd had an abortion four years earlier, and it made me sad. *No, Lord, no baby on that day.*

But as we know, God's plans are not like ours, nor are His thoughts. A painful cramp jolted me out of sleep; I had to use the bathroom. Once I came out, Cedric asked me if I was okay. I said, "I think my labor is starting."

I wasn't ready to go to the hospital. I didn't want to be sent back home. I lay there in bed, slowly tossing and turning during the rest of the night to get comfortable. I would fall asleep between cramps, then wake up again as soon as I felt another. I'm not sure if Cedric went back to sleep because I was more focused on the baby.

When I felt the time was right, I got up and took a quick shower. Cedric got our bags together. I put my dress and sandals on before we headed to the hospital. Cedric seemed excited! All I was thinking about was the exam that I was going to miss and must make up ... dammit!

There was no way this baby was going to wait. My contractions were getting stronger and stronger. I was in active labor.

I wasn't worried about being kicked out of school for missing class as I'd already had a conversation with Dr. Eoff, the associate dean of pharmacy. I promised I would take only two weeks off after birthing the baby and get right back into class. I couldn't miss a beat. My life and children depended on it. The dean was gracious enough to understand. He said to have a safe delivery and not to worry. I didn't have to rush back. But I knew better than that! I was not about to miss the rest of the semester and be put back a year. Oh, no, not me. I was about my goals. My first goal was to graduate in 2009, on time, with the class I started with.

As I walked into the hospital, Cedric was grinning and taking pictures of me. I was not in the mood, but he was camera happy. Once I was admitted, I called my mom to tell her I was in labor. She dropped everything she was doing to come see about her baby. Cedric did his best to make sure I was comfortable. Soon as the nurse started my IV, he started making jokes, trying to make me laugh. He was strategic about it, too. Every time he saw me looking like I was in pain or made a moan, he said something to make me laugh. I was only about three centimeters dilated when Monica, my

Resilient

nurse, asked if I wanted an epidural. I replied with a firm no.

I'm not a fan of needles, let alone a long needle going into my spine. No, thank you! I was happy to receive some pain medication through my IV. The medication had me feeling a little loopy, and my breathing slowed down. So did the baby's heart rate. Monica came into the room, checked the monitors, and put an oxygen mask over my mouth and nose to make sure the baby and I were getting enough oxygen. I also had to change positions to get the baby's heart rate back up. Everything Monica told me to do helped, and we were all relieved.

I was happy to see my mom enter the room. She was smiling from ear to ear. Mom couldn't wait to meet her grandson. Labor was coming along at a steady pace, and the contractions were getting stronger. Soon, I asked for an epidural. I'd said I didn't want one, but this labor was worse than the pain I had with Ariel. Mom was trying to talk me out of it, but I was adamant about receiving the epidural. She whispered something to Monica, but I couldn't figure out what it was. Then, Monica told me she would be back. I patiently waited for her to return with the nurse anesthetist, but it was taking too long.

I asked my mom, "Where is she? How long does it take for them to get the stuff together?" I was agitated and annoyed. The contractions were stronger; they were getting closer together by the minute. When my nurse finally came back in, she checked to see how much more I had dilated. I asked her about the epidural. She looked at me and stated, "It's too late."

I could have shit a brick; I was so mad. I asked about more pain medicine. Monica said it was too late for that too. "You're between seven and eight centimeters."

"It's too late?! How?"

Mama said, "It's for the baby's safety."

Monica saw how aggravated I was, and said, "Try to relax," and left the room.

I was in severe pain. I couldn't eat. I couldn't drink. I couldn't even have ice. I was thirsty, and I was tired. Let's just say I wasn't a peach to be around. I didn't want anybody to talk to me or touch me. I just wanted to lay there in agony until labor was over.

I guess it was taking too long for my water to break, so Monica came in again later to pop my amniotic sac. She checked to see if any meconium was in the fluid. Sure enough, my baby had already had a bowel movement. Monica said, "I'm going to let your doctor know."

Once my water broke, labor really started to pick up. My contractions were back to back now, and before long, I felt like I needed to push. I told my mom. She pushed the button to let the nurse know. Monica came rushing in and checked me. She said, "You're fully dilated," and left the room to alert my doctor.

Moments later, my doctor, Dr. Hamner, walked in with more hospital staff, preparing to deliver my baby. I watched a nurse hold the blue gown open for him as he walked into it and then gloved his hands. I was nervous but ready to get it over with. The pain was unlike any I had ever known.

Before I knew it, the stirrups were up, and I was instructed to scoot down to the edge of the bed. I couldn't move too fast but did as I was told. After I was in position, Dr. Hamner said, "Don't push until I tell you to, kiddo."

"Okay," I said, moaning in pain. My contractions were nonstop, no breaks in between. Cedric stood next to the head of the bed, holding my hand. Mom was standing back, watching, smiling, and waiting. Dr. Hamner stood at the foot of the bed with his arms folded, watching the monitor, gazing back and forth between the monitors and me. Right on time, just as I was feeling a contraction, my doctor said, "Push!"

I bear down. The pain was too much; I started lifting my hips off the bed.

"Kiddo don't come off of the bed. Calm down. Just breathe," he said calmly.

"It hurts!"

Mama came closer to me and said, "Robin, look at me." As I looked at her, she continued, "Breathe with me."

She started inhaling deeply and exhaling slowly. I watched and mimicked her breathing. "It's okay, sweetheart. Now when you push, bear down on your bottom, okay?"

"Okay," I responded, frustrated. I kept breathing slowly and deeply. I kept my eyes on Mama as she returned to where she'd been standing.

"Okay, kiddo. I need you to push," Dr. Hamner chimed in.

I did as I was told, and the pain was almost unbearable. It felt like my vagina was on fire. "You're starting to tear," he said.

I stopped pushing. *So that's why it's so painful. This baby must have a big head.*

I don't know what my doctor was doing down there. By this time, I had gone numb in the vaginal area. "Push!"

I bear down again, then Dr. Hamner asked for suction. "I see his head! Push!"

I bear down again. This time, hoping and praying it was the last push, and it was. *Hallelujah!*

Cedric started crying as he saw our baby boy. I couldn't see him. Dr. Hamner asked Cedric if he wanted to cut the umbilical cord. He stood there crying, shaking his head. Then the first cries of our baby boy filled the room. I was exhausted but thankful he was alive and well. Dr. Hamner handed him to the nurses to be cleaned up and swaddled. Once he was ready, the nurse brought him over and placed him in my arms. *Oh, my God! He is beautiful!*

My eyes watered a little bit (I tried not to be too sentimental) as I looked up at my mama. I forgot all about what was going on down below. I had a vaginal tear, and my doctor was down there stitching me up.

While he was busy working, I looked at my baby boy in awe. "Welcome to the world, Caleb. I've been waiting to meet you." His little eyes were closed and covered with ointment. I finally had my son. I was thankful to God that he was healthy with no birth defects. My big-headed, baby boy was perfect. He was a chunky baby, almost nine pounds, chubby cheeks, fat feet, and fat little fingers. Every time he kicked me or moved, it felt like I was being punched. Now I knew why. I adored him.

Dr. Hamner finished up his work. "Congratulations, kiddo. You have a beautiful boy. I'll be back to check on you tomorrow." Then, he left.

After I had some time to dote on him, the nurses came and took him away for a while. Then Cedric walked out saying that he would be right back. I momentarily wondered where he was going but didn't let it bother me because I was tired anyway.

When Cedric returned, he was holding flowers. He walked over to the bed and set the flowers on the table. Smiling at me, he pulled out a black velvet box, opened it, and there was a beautiful diamond ring. It was the exact ring I saw in the jewelry store. It was princess cut, Victorian style, and exquisite. I had no idea he was going to buy it when I pointed it out to him. I couldn't believe he remembered because it had been a while since he'd seen it. Cedric took it out of the box and said, "I love you. Thank you for bringing my son into the world."

Yes, he said Caleb was his son; that was something else I didn't expect to hear. He tried to put the ring on my finger, but they were still swollen from my pregnancy. I couldn't wait to wear it.

Caleb's white blood cell count was elevated so, we had to stay in the hospital longer than the usual two days. I was worried about him, but the pediatrician assured me that Caleb was on the proper antibiotics and was going to be fine.

When we were finally able to go home, I was relieved. I was tired of being in the hospital. I was ready to be at my home in my bed. Our first night home was like any other night with a newborn. Caleb woke up every two to three hours. To my pleasant surprise, I never had to be awake alone. Cedric was up every time I woke up. Most of the time, he fed Caleb while I went back to sleep. He changed Caleb's diapers and everything without complaint. He loved Caleb as his own. After Caleb turned two weeks old, we took him to his first doctor's appointment. He was still as healthy as could be.

Unfortunately, I had to go back to class. Prior to labor and delivery, Mom agreed to keep Caleb. He wouldn't be old enough to go to daycare when I had to return. I'd done as much breastfeeding as I could to increase my bonding time before my milk dried up.

I was dreading the ride to West Point to drop him off. I didn't want to be away from him, but I didn't have a choice. Caleb remained in West Point with his grandparents and big sister until he was six weeks old.

During those four weeks, we called and checked on him every day. I also drove home every Friday to see my babies. I missed them all the time. Cedric and I had also become inseparable. If I wasn't at his place, he was at mine. We couldn't get enough of each other. It was that fresh and new love with no inhibitions. I loved every moment we spent together. It was like we were written in the stars. I couldn't see any reason why God wouldn't want us to be together. He made me feel like he loved me for who I was and not what he wanted me to be. That was a good feeling. For once, I had someone I could depend on. He'd proven over and over again that I could trust him with my heart, and so I did.

***

I think maybe two or three weeks after Caleb was born, although it could have been longer, I received a phone call from Kent. Kent asked me how I was doing?

"I'm fine, and you?"

"I'm good. How is the baby?"

"He's great. He's beautiful and healthy."

"How much did he weigh?"

"He was almost nine pounds, 20 inches long."

"I miss you."

"Yeah, well, Cedric and I are together now."

"I figured that was going to happen."

"Yep, we're happy."

"Can I see the baby?"

"Yes, you can drive to my parents' house in West Point to see him."

"I don't want to drive to your folks' house. That's a two-hour drive."

"Well, it'll be a two- hour drive for you to come here. What's the difference?" I spat.

"What about a picture? Can you at least send me a picture?"

"Yes, I can e-mail it to you. What's your e-mail address again?" I pretended to write it down. I already had his e-mail address. "Okay, I'll send it to you."

"All right then, bye."

"Bye."

There were a couple of reasons I didn't want Kent to come to my place to see Caleb. The first reason was because he had been an ass my entire pregnancy. He couldn't come sit on my couch and act like we were still friends. The second reason was because I wasn't going to allow him to come and pull the "I'm the father" card on Cedric. Especially since Cedric stepped into the father role for both of my children. I couldn't allow Kent to think for one second he could come back and reclaim his spot like he was father of the year. Some conversations needed to be had. I also didn't want to risk a falling out between Cedric and Kent without having a mediator present. Lastly, Kent needed to meet my parents in an official capacity if he was going to be a part of Caleb's life. There was no time like the present for Kent to officially meet them. But he was a coward. He didn't want to face my parents after the way he'd treated me. I haven't spoken to Kent since that day.

***

Finishing up the fall semester of 2007 after giving birth was a challenge, but not as much as I thought it would be. I made an "A" on the exam I missed due to labor, which was great. I had nothing but time to study the material over and over until I returned to school two weeks later. The second exam for that therapeutics course was a complete one hundred eighty. I made an "F" on it. I had to hurry up and take it so I could go to the next therapeutics block. I didn't get a lot of time to study. I also only attended one lecture for that test. I was behind, but I did what I had to do. Because I made an "A" on the first test, the "F" didn't hurt much. I ended up with a "B-" so I was able to move forward to the next block. There were a lot of late nights and early mornings for the rest of the semester. I studied whenever I could.

Caleb was a good baby. He was sleeping through the night by the time he was two-and-a-half months old, which was a huge blessing. I had prayed repeatedly for God to help me keep up; He undoubtedly had answered my prayers. If it weren't for God, I wouldn't have made it through. Not through high school, not through college, and definitely not through pharmacy school.

Having Cedric in my life was a huge help as well. I wasn't accustomed to having someone help me pay for daycare, milk, diapers, and clothes. As a single mom, all of that fell on me for many years. Don't get me wrong, my mom and Dad doted on Ariel then, and they still do now, but she was still my responsibility. I went to my parents for help only when it was absolutely necessary. I never had to ask them to buy her clothes; it was a given. Mom loved to shop for her. I wasn't going to turn away any help, no matter how it came. But when it came down to rent, lights, gas, water, oil changes, and the like, it was all on me. If I had gone to my parents, I had no doubt they would have given it. But I had to learn to stand on my own. I was raised that way. To have a man ready and willing to help me walk out my journey, without trying to change me or throw my past up in my face, was new to me. I'd never heard a man say, "Don't worry about it," or "I can do this," or "I can do that." All of that was foreign to me. It was a huge adjustment to allow a man to give to me.

In the past, all men had taken from me. None of them added any value to my life. They took value from my life. I was glad to have Cedric love me, but I kept waiting for him to change. It had become second nature to expect the worse out of someone.

We had a christening ceremony for Caleb when he was around two months old. I introduced Cedric to my pastor, Elder Henderson, at Caleb's christening. I wanted April to be there, but she couldn't make it down from Chicago. Cedric stood right there by my side, taking responsibility for my son. Ariel, my sisters, and my parents were there as well.

For the first time, I felt like I was going to have the family unit for my children I'd always wanted. I didn't want to lose that feeling. What bothered me most about it was what would happen if Cedric and I didn't work out. I had my children to think about. By this time, Ariel was already fond of him, and Caleb would grow up knowing him as his father. What if Cedric decided he no longer wanted this life with me one day? What was I going to say to them then? How would I be able to make it better for them?

27

Marriage came up when Caleb was around four months old. Since Cedric and I were together all of the time, he suggested moving in together. Well, I didn't have a problem with that, but I didn't want to live with a man unless I was married. It was just the way I had been raised. I told him how I felt. "We don't have to get married. We can continue dating and living separately. I'm fine with that because we haven't officially been a couple that long."

After giving what I shared some thought, Cedric said, "I want to get married." Although I loved him, I wasn't ready for marriage. I wanted to keep dating for a while. However, he seemed sure. He said, "I want to marry you. I don't want to wait because I don't want to lose you."

I couldn't believe what I was hearing. Why would Cedric think he was going to lose me if we didn't get married? So, I said yes. I didn't see why not. I felt like he was the man for me, and we would be happy together for the rest of our lives.

Eventually, I had a one-on-one talk with Elder Henderson about Cedric. He was quite honest and frank about his thoughts on our relationship. Elder Henderson asked me if I loved Cedric and to tell him about our relationship. I gave every single detail I deemed important, including information about Kent. He said,
"You need to take your time with Cedric. You just had a baby, and you're vulnerable."

Maybe Elder Henderson thought Cedric was playing on my vulnerability, although that's not what he said. He also stated, "Cedric is a good man, but he's not the man God has for you." I didn't like what he said, but I respected his opinion. It could have been God's way of answering my questions about my relationship, or it could have been Elder Henderson's opinion. I didn't know which one of the two were true, but I wasn't ready to let go of the best thing that had happened to me in a long time. I took what Elder Henderson said into consideration, but I decided to take a chance on love to find out where it would take me.

On Friday, February 14, I married my friend and love of my life at the courthouse in Memphis, TN. I was nervous and filled with anxiety that morning. If he was nervous, he hid it quite well. We got up that morning, took Caleb to daycare, and went to class as usual. After classes ended, we went back to the apartment to get dressed up for our small ceremony in the judge's chamber. We drove over together. It took us about twenty minutes to get to our destination. During our drive, I had second thoughts. *Maybe we're rushing into it.*

A lot of people probably would have agreed that we were rushing. I heard Elder Henderson's words, but I ignored them. My instincts were telling me to wait, but I ignored those, too. I knew him well. We had been friends for a long time now. He listened to me, he loved me, he loved my children, he made me feel like I was valued, he would comfort me when I was upset, he was everything and did everything I needed. Maybe that's why I didn't pause to ask him during the drive if he was sure. I didn't want to risk losing him either.

When we got out of the truck, we walked toward the building together, hand in hand. As we walked, I looked at him, and asked, "Are you sure?"

He replied, "Yes, are you?"

No. "Yes," I said, smiling.

We walked in confidently, ready to take on the world together. We went in, said our vows, kissed, and it was official.

As soon as we left the courthouse and got back to the truck, we checked our phones to find that the daycare had called us. We called back to find out what was going on. It turned out, Caleb had a fever. We had to go pick him up. *Seriously?*

We headed to the daycare, still in our wedding attire. We were congratulated by the staff when we walked through the door. We got our baby boy and headed home. A couple we'd grown fond of, Deryk and Yulonda, offered to babysit Caleb for the weekend so we could have a small honeymoon. Initially, they were the only people from our circle of friends in Memphis who knew we'd gotten married. We packed Caleb up and headed downtown to take him to their place.

We spent the weekend at Embassy Suites, reeling in from what we'd just done. At least I know I was. I couldn't believe I had gotten married, especially without my family knowing.

We just went and did it. We threw caution to the wind and moved forward, hoping everything would work out for the best. I didn't want to be without him, and he didn't want to be without me. I was his love, and he was mine. That's all we knew. Looking back, I can see we went into our marriage without a plan. We didn't discuss finances or how we would raise our children. We didn't discuss what church we would go to or in what direction we were headed. I asked him about going to marriage counseling before we got married, but he said we didn't need it. All we needed was each other and to communicate. It didn't seem like a big deal; I let it slide. Hindsight is 20/20.

It wasn't long after we got married that we started having a little bit of conflict, a conflict I wanted to resolve. But he wanted to ignore and sweep it under the rug. Cedric was changing Caleb's diaper one evening while we were taking a break from studying. I heard a loud slap, and then Caleb wailed out in pain. I jumped up from my seat and turned to see what was going on?

"Did you just hit him?"

"Yeah, he peed on me while I was changing his diaper. He knows better than that!"

"What?! He is a baby! Babies pee whenever they feel like it!"

"This is my son, and nobody is going to tell me how to raise my child."

"He is our son, and we will raise him together!"

"You don't see nobody else here helping you, do you?"

There it was! He slyly threw my past in my face. He made me feel so small. But I still had to stand up for my baby, my Caleb. "Don't you ever hit him again! He's still a baby! He's not a toddler you're trying to teach right from wrong." But he kept hitting Caleb. It got to the point where I wanted to be the only one who would change his diaper, bathe him, and feed him. I didn't want Cedric to touch him.

What bothered me no longer mattered to him, but anything that bothered him did matter to me. Every time I wanted to discuss something going on, he would shut it down and wouldn't discuss it any further. I was disturbed by this, but he felt as long he was contributing to the bills being paid and remained a "provider," then everything was all right and would work itself out. I disagreed. I needed a partner, not a master. I knew then that I should have listened to the Holy Spirit and not have gotten married. However, through all of this, I still loved him, and I knew he loved me. Our disconnect had already begun, but instead of tucking my tail and asking for an annulment, I chose to stay in it and fight for my marriage because I made the commitment. I wanted to give our union a fair chance.

Besides our disagreements at home, I also wasn't feeling "the love" from some of his family. I'm sure they felt like he deserved to be with someone who didn't come with children. The way they treated me made me feel that way for certain. They would speak to me, and that would be it. I could tell that it was a struggle for them to connect with my children. I wasn't very comfortable around them. They didn't publicly acknowledge me, nor did they welcome me into their family with open arms. I don't know if they thought I was using Cedric or not, but that wasn't the case.

Cedric was not my savior. Jesus was and still is. Cedric didn't find me on the street, needing to be rescued. I most certainly was not a damsel in distress. I was a pharmacy student trying to live out my dreams. What I didn't have, my parents had more than enough to give to help with my children when I made my needs known. I was never alone. Not only because I had the support from my parents if I ever called them, but because I knew where my help ultimately came from. The Lord had proven Himself strong in my life over and over. He had never failed me. Before I would ask my parents for anything, I called God first. So even if there were no Cedric, I would be all right and so would my children. Since his family knew the circumstances surrounding my pregnancy and the fact that I already had a daughter, I was looked down upon. It was no secret to me how they felt about me. I saw it in the spirit. I heard it in the fake hellos and goodbyes, but I didn't say a word. I had become accustomed to this type of treatment, anyway.

Yes, it hurt my feelings, but there was nothing I could do or say to make them feel otherwise. Cedric's mom, however, was kind and loving toward my children and me. So were his big brother and sister-in-law. They did what they could to make me and my children feel comfortable. For that, I was appreciative.

**

While Cedric and I were navigating marriage and parenthood, we still managed to survive pharmacy school. There was a lottery for our last year-and-a-half of school. Some of the students would have to either stay in Memphis or go to Knoxville or Nashville to complete their rotations. I didn't have to enter the lottery because I had children, but Cedric had to enter the lottery. It was just our luck that he was going to be sent to Knoxville, but he was able to get out of it and remain in Memphis with me, thank God.

Our rotations every month consisted of rounding with doctors, pharmacists, and other pharmacy students. We also had presentations and journal clubs to do. It might seem like it wasn't a lot of work, but it was. We had to have our game face on every day, ready to answer random questions, and do whatever we had to do to satisfy our preceptors. Each month, there was a different preceptor, hospital, disease state, or area of pharmacy to focus on. I learned a lot during this time. Those experiences are some I won't ever forget. I had a rotation at St. Jude Children's Hospital (where I cried every day for a week), LeBonheur Children's Hospital, Baptist Women's Hospital, and more. My primary interests were oncology and pediatrics. I requested rotations in those areas. I had rotations in ambulatory care, cardiology, nutrition, and drug information as well, but I enjoyed pediatrics and oncology the most.

We were allowed to choose a month off during our rotations. Cedric and I chose to have the month of February off. I told Cedric that I wanted to have a wedding. I figured we could use our same rings from our first ceremony, but Cedric had quite a surprise for me. I was talking on the phone to him like I usually did while heading home. He said he was looking for another ring for me, which I was completely against. We couldn't afford it. Besides, I was satisfied with the ring I already had, the ring he'd given me when I gave birth to Caleb. I loved that ring. I still love that ring.

Anyway, after absolutely forbidding him to buy it, I put my key in the door to unlock it. As soon as I walked in, he was there on one knee with the ring box opened with the most sincere, loving look in his eyes. He said, "Robin, I love you more than anything. Will you marry me?" I was stunned.

"What are you doing?" I asked with glee. "We are already

married!" I couldn't stop smiling.

"I know, but this is the ring I want you to have. This is what you deserve." I looked at the ring. It was a beautiful ring with three round-cut diamonds. The center diamond was larger than the other two on either side, and it had diamond banquettes on each side. It was stunning. I looked at him with so much love. As mad as I wanted to be at him for spending so much money, I couldn't be.

"Yes, I'll marry you, again and again," I said with teary eyes. He took the ring I was wearing off of my left ring finger and put it on my right hand. Then, he slid my new ring on, and it was perfect. We kissed and hugged. I couldn't stop smiling. He later told me *that* was the proposal he'd wanted to give me before we got married. He just wanted to make it right. Well, I was certainly surprised. It was completely unexpected.

We had our wedding ceremony on February 14, 2009, at my church in Starkville, MS. Elder Henderson performed the ceremony for us. Everything didn't go as perfectly as I had planned, but it was still beautiful. The colors were crimson red and ivory. I did my best to make the wedding as personalized as possible. I bought monogrammed napkins for the reception, an ivory aisle runner with our names on it, and the Bible verse, "I am my beloved's, and my beloved is mine," a sterling silver cutlery set for us to cut the cake with, a blinged-out letter "P" as the cake topper, a personalized unity candle, and wine glasses. I also used the voiceover from Tyler Perry's movie, *Madea's Family Reunion*. It was Maya Angelou reciting the poem, "In and Out of Time."

As I held my dad's hand and walked down the aisle toward Cedric, I gazed at him and knew that despite all of our issues, I wanted to spend the rest of my life loving him. We said our vows.

Then, Elder Henderson prayed for our family. Cedric and I walked back down the aisle hand in hand, smiling from ear to ear.

Our reception was beautiful. The wedding planner decorated the venue just as I would have. I had a candy table with a chocolate fountain for the fruit, a dessert table with monogrammed to-go containers and napkins, another table was set up for the buffet-style dinner; the guests could walk on both sides to fill their plates, the lighting was beautiful, and all of the tables were decorated beautifully with flowers, rose petals, and large centerpieces. I loved it.

Although our wedding cake tasted delicious, I didn't like the way it was decorated. I wanted it to be all white, but for some reason, the designer added red icing, something I didn't even ask for. However, I enjoyed the reception. I changed out of my wedding dress into a white satin dress that I bought for the reception so I could relax and enjoy myself without pulling my wedding dress around. I danced with my husband, my dad, and my line sisters. Cedric and I danced to *At Last* by Etta James. Cedric is not the best dancer, but he was able to sway from side to side as he danced with me. Having him in my arms was like heaven. I loved him so much and I wanted our marriage to work. I prayed to God that everything between us would be greater with time.

I loved the dance with my dad. It was the dance I had always dreamed of. We danced to *Your Joy* by Chrisette Michele. I absolutely love that song. The first time I heard it, I knew that no matter when I got married, I was going to dance with my father to that song. I cried as he held me in his arms. For just a moment, I was his little girl again. When our dance was over, he dried my eyes with his handkerchief and escorted me off the dance floor. Cedric danced with his mom and my mom. His mom was as beautiful as could be and she looked so happy. My mama had it going on too, and my dad was as handsome as ever in his tuxedo. By the end of the night, Cedric and I were both tired, but we still managed to have some fun when we got back to our hotel room.

For our honeymoon, Cedric's brother gifted us a trip to the Virgin Islands, one of the most beautiful places I'd ever laid eyes on. The water was crystal blue, the sky was clear, and the temperature was perfect every day we were there. Cedric's dad and stepmom had given us a thousand dollars as a gift since our rehearsal dinner had been ruined. The restaurant gave away our reserved space because we were late getting there after the wedding rehearsal. I was disappointed in how that turned out; at least we got a thousand dollars as a result of not having the dinner. We used that money to spend on our honeymoon, so we wouldn't have to use so much of our money. We were able to do a couple of excursions and go on a sunset cruise. We had the time of our lives. Because Ariel and Caleb were with my parents, we didn't worry too much about them.

After about four days of the Caribbean, I started missing home. Although the islands were practically magical, and I didn't want my honeymoon to end, I was ready to get home to my babies. Cedric had his way of helping me relax and not worry much about getting home. We were in the Caribbean for six nights and seven days, which was the longest I'd ever been away from home.

***

When the honeymoon was over, we had to head back to school to complete our last two rotations. That time flew by. Before we knew it, it was time to plan for our graduation. I went to the registrar's office to hyphenate my name. I'd never planned to drop my surname under any circumstances, not even for marrying the love of my life. I'd worked hard to achieve so much as Robin Terry; I wasn't going to give it up. Cedric was understanding of that. After all, he knew there was no changing my mind. We received our cap and gowns and took pictures for the yearbook a couple of months or so before graduation. Our hooding ceremony was the day before graduation. The hooding ceremony was when it all began sinking in that I was going to be graduating. When that hood was placed over my head and around my neck, I was a step closer to becoming Dr. Robin Terry. On the inside, I was screaming with excitement.

    I woke up excited on graduation day. All of my family as well as April came to town. For some reason, it seemed as if April didn't want to be there. She didn't appear to be excited for me at all. She was very quiet and stand-offish. It hurt my feelings, but I didn't let it ruin my day. I was happy to see the smile on my dad's face. It warmed my heart to know I'd made him proud. He was so ecstatic that he offered to cover the licensing fees for Cedric and me. There was no way we were going to turn that money down. The costs of those national and state license exams were expensive. My mom expressed how she was proud that I'd overcome obstacles and setbacks to make it to where I was that day. There were a lot of tears, but they were tears of joy.

    By the grace of God, I had done it! I had done what the naysayers said I couldn't do. I had become the opposite of what the they said I would be. I accomplished everything I had set out to do despite heartbreak, difficulties, rejection, disappointment, hurt, setbacks, and deception. For a fifteen-year-old pregnant girl to graduate eleven years later with a doctorate, not having failed one class or be dismissed from school for any reason, was a victorious and humbling experience. I had to keep going. I couldn't stop. I wouldn't stop.

UTHSC's graduation was held on May 29, 2009 at FedEx Forum in Memphis, TN. I graduated with over six hundred other students, including students from the College of Nursing, College of Medicine, College of Allied Health Sciences, College of Dentistry, and College of Graduate Health Sciences. I'm not sure what their stories were or how they felt about their future endeavors. But I was filled with joy and anticipation. I was filled with gratefulness. I was grateful for how far I'd come, for how far God had brought me.

When my name was called, and I walked across that stage to accept my Doctor of Pharmacy degree from The University of Tennessee Health Science Center, I wanted to do a cartwheel and dance my way from one side to the other. However, to keep from embarrassing myself and my parents, I smiled and shouted, "Glory to God!" with my whole heart and soul from within. When that degree was placed in my hands, I said, "Thank You, Jesus!"

Resilient

To be continued...

God's Glory

I eventually began to understand my worth. I began to understand what April had been trying to tell me all along. She would tell me all the time that it was like I didn't believe I deserved everything God had for me. The fact of the matter was that I didn't believe it. I had made so many mistakes along the way; I thought my chances were slim to none. Honestly, I didn't even fully understand why God would even want to deal with me. I was a misfit. I didn't fit in with a lot of people around me, and I didn't quite fit in at church either. But even in the midst of all of my unwise decisions, God still had his hand on my life. Even when I didn't know I needed to be kept, He still kept me. Every time I went the wrong way, I could feel the tugging and nudging in my spirit to go back His way. I would always go back because once I had made a mess of things, it was only God who could pull me through. He was always there waiting and ready with open arms to receive me. A lot of times, I felt like Paul with a thorn in my flesh, tormented by my faults, knowing that only God could give me the peace I longed for.

I knew from reading the Word of God that He wants for His children to live a life full of joy and abundance, but it seemed to be just out of my reach for a long time. I had to consistently say, "I believe God," and "I trust You, Lord." *Sometimes we have to faith it until we make it.* I learned to do just that. As I matured in Christ, every time the enemy came and tried to steal what little bit of faith and hope I had, I chose to praise God and focus on Him instead. So, my faith grew instead of dwindled. *You know, sometimes that is hard to do when your back is against the wall, and it seems like nothing is going to work out. But once God has proven Himself to you, that is all you need to know; He can and will do it again. He will do it from faith to faith and from glory to glory if only you believe.* Amid my believing, I consistently worked on walking in righteousness. I know I'm not perfect, and I never will be. But I work on it every single day. Even today, life has thrown me quite a few curveballs. A lot of things I didn't see coming. I've had more heartache and pain, as well as tough choices to make. I was a good girl gone bad for awhile due to some of life's circumstances. I've again contemplated suicide and suffered from depression, but I'm still here. I'm still here to tell you this story. I'm still here to tell you that God is still good. He is still able. He is still a very present help in the time of trouble. He is still your joy and peace. He is whatever you need Him to be for you. I'm a witness to that. I am so happy to be alive right now. The enemy can no longer taunt me. I can finally say that I have conquered my past. I'm no longer held prisoner to it. I owe all of my growth and everything I've learned to God. He was and still is my teacher. Let Him teach you! Let Him love you! Let Him save you!

Afterword

When people ask me how I did it, I give all the honor and glory to God because it was all God. It was by His grace, love, mercy, persistence, and devotion to me that I was able to face everything and go through it all without failing. God never failed me, not once. I owe everything I am to Him. To God be the glory!

It is my prayer that this book touches the lives of young girls and women all over the world. I began writing my story when I was 30 years old. I was praying and asking God what my divine assignment is. I initially thought pharmacy was my be all and end all. But pharmacy wasn't fulfilling. I still felt like there was something else I was supposed to be doing with my life. The voice I heard while lying on the floor when I was nineteen years old kept coming back to my remembrance. I had no interest in preaching. I'm a shy introvert around strangers. I didn't feel comfortable trying to tell someone else to live right when I had done so many wrong things.

After praying one day, I heard God say, "Write a book." I wasn't sure I wanted to do that. Write about what? I'm a private person. I don't want to tell the world my business. I jotted down some ideas, still not wanting to write about myself. I remembered that I happened to share some things that I had gone through with Lillie one day when we were talking. This was before I turned thirty. She said, "Girl you need to write a book." I didn't consider it. After I turned thirty, I was in church and the pastor said, "God has told somebody to write a book. That book needs to be written." The pastor was on my street when he said that, but I still didn't want to do it. I didn't have time. I had young children and I was working. I was more focused on being a wife and mother than anything. Despite my efforts to avoid it, God kept speaking to me.

In 2012, I sat down to start writing my story, I didn't have a title. I didn't know exactly where I was going to go with it. I asked God where to start and where to stop. I made an outline and started typing. Then I stopped. I started crying because I didn't want to relive my past. I had to unpack the pain I had boxed up so long ago. I didn't want to feel any of it. I didn't pick my assignment back up until 2014. I started writing, but then I stopped again; again because of the pain I had to deal with. I put it back down. I picked it back up in 2016. I started writing, but then put it on hold just long enough to start my nonprofit foundation called Illustrious Adolescent Mother, Inc. I also enrolled in the Master of Business Administration program at University of Memphis. I started out taking only one class at a time so I could focus on the book as well.

Then my marriage fell apart. I put the book down again. It was all too much for me to deal with. I was devastated. As a result, I ended up going down a road I was never meant to travel. Between 2016 and 2018, my life was a rollercoaster. There was no way I could finish writing my story. I had new hurt on top of old hurt. When I attempted to write, I was writing in anger. I had to delete a lot and start over. When January 2019 rolled around, God said, "Finish this year." I said, "Yes, Lord." I spent every free moment I had writing. I stayed up late and got up early just as I had done when I was working toward higher education. I did what I had to do to complete my divine assignment.

I don't know what is to come after this book is published. I don't know how it will sell. I don't even know if anybody will bother to pick it up and read it. But I do know, I want my story to inspire and encourage other young ladies like me. The misfits. The risk-takers. The headstrong. The kind-hearted. The fighters. The survivors. When I was almost done with my story, I still didn't have a title. I said, "Lord, I need just one word that describes who I am. That one word will be the title of the book." Then, I heard "Resilient." That's how I got the title of this book. Resilient. It's my story, but God's glory.

***

Stay in Touch with Me…

I have a lot to offer to empower teens and young mothers. You can follow me on social media and my website:

Facebook: Facebook.com/dr.robinterry
Twitter: @dvinediamond
Instagram: @dvinediamond
Website: https://www.robinterry.me

Acknowledgments

First giving honor to God, who is the King and God of everything. It is because of You, God, that I am. I thank God for all He has done in my life and for everything He is going to do. I thank my parents for all the support they have given me through the years. Mama and Daddy, I love you so much! There is no way I would be where I am today without my village. I thank my sisters and best friend for always being supportive. I love you all very much. To all of my line sisters, I love you! I appreciate all of my relatives and close friends who showed love and support through those adolescent, tough years. Thank you, Ms. Barbara Joe, for taking on the task of editing my book. You've taught me a lot about being a writer. I look forward to working with you again on my next project. I also want to thank all of the men who have come and gone; it's because of you that I have great writing material ☺.

www.ingramcontent.com/pod-product-compliance
Lightning Source LLC
Chambersburg PA
CBHW020357080526
44584CB00014B/1057